Team Traps

Preface

━━━━━━━━━━━━━ ❧ ❧ ❧ ❧ ━━━━━━━━━━━━━

When I began my consulting work in the early 1980s, only a few organizations were experimenting with what we commonly called, in those days, "participative management." Though few in number, the pioneers of that era were already demonstrating the superiority of team-based workplaces. Side-by-side comparisons in the manufacture of everything from pet food to computer chips pointed to the same conclusion: Participative, team-based organizations were more productive, more adaptive, and less costly; they produced better quality and developed employees who were more loyal and committed than their traditionally managed counterparts.

Today, virtually every major corporation has a team experiment underway. The same is true among government, nonprofit, and academic institutions. And no longer are these innovative work practices concentrated in manufacturing settings. Financial companies, dealerships, sales organizations, software houses, marketing groups, and engineering firms are all jumping on the team bandwagon with the zeal of revolutionaries. It is now universally accepted that the high-performing organizations of the coming century will be those that most effectively unleash the intellectual, problem-solving, and decision-making abilities of their only appreciable asset—their people.

Organizational Quicksand

To create a high-performing team, leaders must be prepared for a long and difficult journey. This is particularly true in our current generation where virtually every corporation, agency, and institution remains dominated by traditional management. Leaders face the double challenge of overcoming systems, roles, and processes that work against team development and are deeply embedded in the work culture of the very organization they are trying to transform, and, simultaneously, attempting to address the interpersonal, conflict, and group dynamic complexities inherent in forming teams. The route is difficult—as every step is taken, there is the potential for the effort to disappear into a sinkhole or for the team to become trapped in organizational quicksand. For team leaders and team members alike, many hard lessons have to be learned.

The Hard Lessons the Easy Way

Some managers and consultants argue that hard lessons can only be learned the hard way; they say the pains of personal experience are the only teacher. This viewpoint is really more a rationalization than a philosophy. It is as silly as thinking that we can only become aware of the potential dangers of fire after we have been burned by an open flame. All it takes to learn the hard lessons the easy way is a willingness to study and learn from the experiences of others.

Team Traps has been written to help team leaders and team members learn hard lessons the easy way. The chapters are filled with examples of the common traps that hurt team effectiveness, as told by those who saw the traps firsthand. Although I have used pseudonyms to mask the identities of the people and companies involved, have changed physical locations, and, admittedly, have taken some literary license to help amplify key points, each case study that is presented in Chapters 3 through

11 is based on an actual event that was experienced by members of a real team. By studying and learning from their experiences, clear strategies and tactics will emerge that can help us toward avoidance of the common pitfalls that have proved destructive to so many teams.

STEVEN R. RAYNER

Freeland, Washington

Contents

꣠꣠ ꣠꣠ ꣠꣠ ꣠꣠

Part I

Warning Signs

Chapter 1

The End of Camelot

In the autumn of 1988, Tektronix held the first public conference ever sponsored by a major corporation on the topic of employee involvement. Of particular interest to the over 500 participants attending the three-day session was the extraordinary story of the Tektronix portable oscilloscope division. The division, after sustaining a brutal attack from overseas competition in the early 1980s, had fought back, regaining market share and profitability. In a two-year period, the division went from being the company's number-one loser (last among Tektronix's 29 divisions, with a $23 million loss on $170 million in sales) to a rating as its premier group. The secret to success, according to Fred Hanson, the division's vice president at that time, was remarkably simple: Get your people involved.

And people were involved. An operator on the manufacturing line in the portables division could stop production if he or she discovered a quality problem. Line workers could redesign the entire process flow if it would lead to improved performance; they regularly took telephone calls directly from customers; and they provided performance feedback to peers. In new product development efforts, cross-functional teams—with representatives from engineering, manufacturing, marketing, finance, and human resources—were formed. The time frame for product development was immediately reduced from four years to two. With more "wild experimentation"—a strongly encouraged trait of the team-based work culture—design teams soon had new products rolling out in less than 18 months.

Many onlookers were astounded by the success the portables division had achieved and were anxious to replicate it. The Vancouver, Washington, facility became overrun with tours, serving as a source of inspiration for a number of senior managers from companies such as Martin Marietta, Allied Signal, Texas Instruments, TRW, and Fisher Controls.

The Decline and Downfall

Today, the portables division no longer exists due to a massive consolidation effort. Nearly all of the senior managers who were part of the turnaround have long since left Tektronix. Even the Vancouver facility is gone—operated, ironically, by a Tektronix competitor.

The experience of the portables division is by no means unique. Digital Equipment Corporation's (DEC) Enfield, Connecticut, plant, once referred to as the "Mecca of new organization design," was shut down during a consolidation effort. The plant was one of the most publicized and well-documented examples of a team-based work system in action—a book and countless articles had described its innovative management approach. When the shutdown was announced, DEC received over 1,000 letters, from people all over the United States who had either toured or read about the facility, requesting that the plant be kept open.

Martin Marietta's Space Launch Systems group, which, in a mere 18 months, documented a savings of more than $10 million through its employee involvement efforts, saw its attempts to transform the organization begin to stumble when layoffs were announced.

The list could go on and on. There are any number of examples of highly effective organizations (with well-documented performance results that spanned years) that no longer exist. What happened? How could a large organization, once so effective, collapse so quickly and so completely?

The Team Advantage?

Critics are quick to cite these examples as illustrative of how team-based work systems simply don't work. Advocates of this perspective see the need for a return to the essential features of traditional management—direct management control over work processes, decision making, and problem solving; narrowly defined work roles; thick policy and procedure manuals to manage by; clear boundaries between departments; and a rigid chain of command. This dying perspective holds on to the view that if we control better, we manage better.

The problem with this argument is that it ignores what has been achieved by countless organizations that have embraced team-based work systems. Those close to the Tektronix effort agree that the emphasis on a team-based work culture was the key component in its extraordinary turnaround. Quality at DEC's Enfield plant was so good that no traditionally structured organization has ever been able to replicate it. Martin Marietta's Space Launch Systems group documented cost savings far beyond what had ever been achieved using "old style" management. Procter & Gamble (P&G), Goodyear, Kodak, IBM, ABB, and Monsanto are but a few additional examples of companies that have seen the dramatic impact of the new management perspective. The conclusions of recent studies by the Department of Labor and the Center for Effective Organizations have empirically confirmed what organizations in both the public and private sectors have been claiming for over a decade—empowered work teams produce superior results.

The question is not whether teams can work—they can and usually do when systematically put in place with strong management support, adequate resources, clear focus, and sufficient training and development. Yet, a variety of factors can conspire to assassinate even the most carefully planned and effectively implemented team efforts.

Despite the many team failures that have occurred over the past decade, there have been few attempts to examine the details of what happened. How can a team that has demonstrated extraordinary performance for years suddenly dissolve? What are the common pitfalls and traps that can lead a team to extinction?

Camelot Revisited

The most interesting organizations to examine are those that have had some of the most spectacular successes and most dramatic crashes. Their stories touch us in much the same way as does the story of King Arthur. We marvel at the remarkable creation of Camelot, but its decline and downfall ignite our fascination. By the story's end, we can clearly see how a few key events transformed Camelot from a utopian kingdom to a vacant wasteland.

The corporate Camelots—like Tektronix, DEC, and Martin Marietta—all have a number of common characteristics:

■ There had been widespread effort to create high-performing teams throughout an entire division or an entire plant.

■ Each company had invested a tremendous amount in employee training and development.

■ Information, including data that had previously been considered "management confidential," was openly shared with all employees.

■ The teams were actively involved in redesigning work flow and processes to improve productivity, quality, and cost performance.

■ Employee morale was very high.

■ The teams that were in place had been highly successful, demonstrating levels of performance that had been unattainable—arguably, even unimaginable—under traditional management practices.

■ Despite considerable long-term success and a strong team-based work culture, the team philosophy ended abruptly, in just a few months.

The Megatraps

Each of these organizations was the victim of a megatrap. A megatrap is a problem that ultimately swallows up teaming efforts in entire plants or divisions—or even entire companies. Once trapped, the struggling organization sees its effectiveness spiral downward. And, as Tektronix, DEC, and Martin Marietta experienced, even the most successful organizations can fall prey. As shown in Figure 1.1, the megatraps are:

1. Strategic blunder.
2. Inability to transfer learning.
3. Collision of work cultures.

Strategic Blunder

No organizational structure is immune to the strains and pressures of market conditions, competitive threats, or technological change, regardless of how well its internal management structure operates. High employee involvement is not a single-dose elixir that will help organizations overcome all of their woes. This point became painfully clear to People Express airlines during the 1980s. Having the most highly participative organization in the airline industry meant little in light of a major strategic error: failing to go after the business traveler market. In the end, having a highly involved workforce that was the envy of its competitors could scarcely improve the company's financial position. Teams cannot cover-up for bad fundamentals or strategic blunders.

Inability to Transfer Learning

Managers tend to discount the successes of others as being flukes or to explain them as the result of rare and unique circumstances. In organizations, there is even a name for this phenomenon: "the not-invented-here syndrome." A former production manager at Procter & Gamble's highly innovative Lima, Ohio, plant recounts how, in the 1960s, shortly after the plant start-up, Lima's success was viewed by other P&G managers to be a result of its superior technology. By the 1970s, with the equipment clearly aging but plant performance still 30 to 40

Figure 1.1   The Three Megatraps

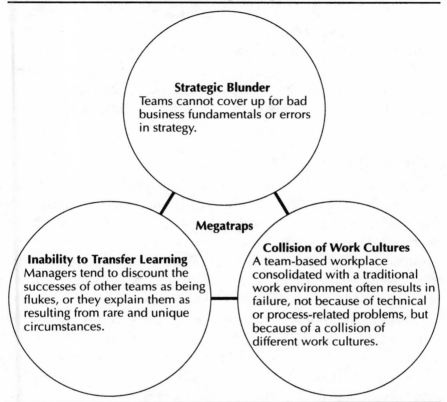

Strategic Blunder
Teams cannot cover up for bad business fundamentals or errors in strategy.

Megatraps

Inability to Transfer Learning
Managers tend to discount the successes of other teams as being flukes, or they explain them as resulting from rare and unique circumstances.

Collision of Work Cultures
A team-based workplace consolidated with a traditional work environment often results in failure, not because of technical or process-related problems, but because of a collision of different work cultures.

percent better than comparable facilities, the focus shifted to the workforce. The people at Lima had been, the argument went, handpicked, and the facility was nonunionized. Not until the 1980s was there a real understanding of how much the management system—with its emphasis on teamwork and involvement—had contributed to the bottom-line results.

The tendency to dismiss what are often significant achievements hampers both the credibility and the assumed relevance of employee involvement. The most innovative teams are rarely found at corporate headquarters. Rather, they are on the periphery, either at remote sites or in small, isolated units. Typically, the management of these units has limited ability to influence corporate-level change that would be advantageous to the ongoing team-development efforts. A host of policies, procedures, processes, and systems form substantial and aggravating barriers that consume tremendous amounts of time, energy, and patience.

Collision of Work Cultures

Consolidation efforts often have a crippling effect on team development—not good news during an era in which restructuring has become commonplace. The problem is not so much the restructuring per se, but the careless manner in which many consolidation decisions are made. Typically, consolidation occurs without consideration of the work cultures of the groups that are being combined. A mismatch can prove particularly negative to high-involvement teams, which will tend to view the consolidation as a demonstration of management's lack of commitment to the teaming philosophy. Changes to the team's charter and membership—activities that typically accompany consolidations—will likely lead to a regression in its overall operating effectiveness. Many consolidation efforts have ended in failure, not because of technical or process-related problems, but because very different work cultures and work experiences collided.

Perhaps an even worse scenario is created when the consolidation announcement is used as the mechanism to introduce a new team-based work system. The McDonnell-Douglas Commercial Airplane Division ventured down this slippery slope when it announced—to an audience of more than 5,000 managers—that, under its new Total Quality Management System (TQMS), the company would need 1,000 fewer managers.

Spreading salt on the wound, the company informed the managers that they would have to reapply and survive a rigorous selection process if they hoped to land one of the remaining management positions. The alternative for those who didn't get selected was clear—a layoff notice.

In the months that followed, there was utter chaos. One manager described how he regularly went for weeks not knowing whom he was supposed to be reporting to. Another McDonnell-Douglas employee noted that he had no fewer than five different managers during the course of the year immediately following the announcement. The whole idea of teams and quality management was met with widespread cynicism (understandably, given the circumstances). For many employees, TQMS came to stand for "Time to Quit and Move to Seattle" (the home of McDonnell-Douglas's arch rival, Boeing).

Although strategic blunders, poorly planned reorganizations, and the epidemic of the not-invented-here syndrome have led to some sensational failures, they are far from the most common traps facing teams. The megatraps, which predominantly afflict large organizations (100 or more persons), represent a fraction of the trip wires facing teams. The most pervasive traps—and arguably the most damaging—are the ones lurking in the hallways, offices, shop floors, and conference rooms of small work teams everywhere. They are the team traps.

Chapter 2

─────────── ❧❧❧❧ ───────────

Teaming with Traps

Experimentation with team-based work systems has exploded over the past decade—so much so that it has now become accepted that the preeminent organizations of the future will use teams as the primary work unit. Classic management, with its emphasis on separating people into narrowly defined jobs, having centralized management control, and maintaining a rigid chain of command, is quickly becoming as much a vestige of the past as the horse-drawn carriage.

A recent study commissioned by the Association for Quality and Participation (AQP) found that 68 percent of Fortune 1000 companies planned to increase their use of team-based work systems. Perhaps an even more extraordinary statistic was the percentage of companies that planned to lessen their use of teams—barely 1 percent.

Despite the widespread acceptance that team-based work systems produce vastly superior results, most employee involvement efforts are still occurring in relatively small, often isolated units. The majority of newly formed teams reside in pilot groups—specially chosen "experimental" teams with as few as 5 to 15 members. Although each year brings a new list of corporations and government agencies that are attempting to spread the team philosophy organizationwide, large-scale implementations like Corning's Blacksburg facility or companywide efforts like those at Nucor Steel remain the exception rather than the rule. The dominant strategy is to experiment with a few pilot teams, monitor the results, and delicately expand the effort to other parts of the organization.

The small teams that are formed are often operating as an island surrounded by a sea of traditional (and often counterteam) management practices. Such teams are prime candidates for becoming trapped. Often they have idealistic intentions but lackluster management support. Because these teams are not viewed as part of a comprehensive, organizationwide change process, their resources, information, and training are often limited.

Across North America, thousands of these small teams are being formed each year. With the number of new teams rapidly growing in organizations that are still predominantly governed by a traditional management philosophy, obvious questions emerge: How many of these teams will be successful? How many will ultimately fail?

Identifying Team Traps

Although estimates vary widely, the most compelling evidence suggests that nearly 40 percent of all newly created teams will fail to produce the results that were anticipated. In most cases, that translates to little or no discernible improvement—a far cry from the 30 to 40 percent productivity gains

often cited in the literature as common among successful implementations. The reason for the discrepancy? Teams that
don't live up to their potential often hit trip wires that—if recognized and understood—could have been avoided.

A team trap can be defined as:

> An initial problem, issue, or mere annoyance that members of a team
> (usually 5 to 15 persons) face, which, if left unchecked, leads to a
> sharp decline in team performance.

Team traps are highly deceptive because what may seem like a
relatively trivial issue—such as delaying a team decision—can
have disastrous consequences (e.g., a missed market opportunity
worth hundreds of thousands of dollars). For this reason, it is important to recognize, long before the full fury of any impact is felt,
the early warning signs that indicate a trap has been tripped.

These early signs will be familiar to nearly anyone who has
been frustrated during a poorly run meeting or has left work ex-
asperated at how long it was taking a team to make a simple decision. Few teams practice the disciplines that can ultimately
lead to immunity. For most teams, all it takes to trigger a trap is
a short lapse in leadership, out-of-focus priorities, or a lack of
capability and skill development.

The Common Traps

Although literally hundreds of traps can open a gateway to
team disaster, the relatively small subset shown in Figure 2.1 rep-
resents the most common traps. Each is discussed briefly here.

Leader Abdication

Some managers, in their sincere efforts to be good team leaders, make a serious mistake: they withdraw from their group and

Figure 2.1 The Common Team Traps

- Leader abdication
- Successionless planning
- Downsizing
- Political suicide
- Team arrogance
- Undefined accountability
- Short-term focus
- Disruptive team member
- Poor teamwork habits
- Decision by default
- Varied team-member contributions
- Participation gimmickry

consciously avoid interacting with team members. They wrongly assume that the best way they can help the team become more self-directed is by personally becoming less involved.

Successionless Planning

The important role that one individual—a champion for change—can play in developing a high-performance team is often underestimated. If a team is newly formed or still in relative infancy, losing its leader to a transfer, a promotion, a new job, or retirement can mark the beginning of the team's demise—particularly if the replacement brings in a management philosophy that runs counter to team development.

Downsizing

A decision to downsize as a way of shoring up short-term profits can destroy all the loyalty and commitment created by years of team development. The end result—as disgruntled workers look for new opportunities—can be a great "brain drain."

Political Suicide

Companies, government agencies, academic institutions, and even nonprofit organizations are inherently political. Ignoring or defying the organization's political side can lead to some harsh consequences, particularly if those in power are publicly challenged or ridiculed by over zealous team members.

Team Arrogance

A team can become so focused on achieving its own goals that it does not consider the impact its actions may have on other groups or organizations. Outsiders see the team as arrogant and ruthless. Insiders see the team as effective and misunderstood. Overall, the team's belief in its own superiority has a detrimental effect on the performance of the organization as a whole.

Undefined Accountability

In this trap, a team may regularly make decisions on which no subsequent action is ever taken. Members are then frustrated by the collective lack of accountability. In instances when action is taken and the execution is poor or a mistake is made, no one takes responsibility. It is rarely clear who is accountable for specific action items, and when an action item is designated as the responsibility of the entire team, nothing happens.

Short-Term Focus

Failure to see the "big picture" can lead a team to pursue strategies and make decisions that help pump up its own performance numbers but leave the rest of the organization in shambles. Not having the information that allows seeing the forest rather than the trees can lead to suspect plans and poorly reasoned decisions.

Disruptive Team Member

A disruptive member who is not dealt with firmly and effectively can damage the performance of the entire team. The reluctance of team members to provide direct and honest feedback to a peer can lead to frustration and declining performance.

Poor Teamwork Habits

When a team operates as a group of individuals rather than as a tight, cohesive unit, little, if any, synergy is created when team members collaborate on projects. Meetings tend to be ineffective, with members often not showing up or coming in late. The feeling of the majority is: "My real work is too important for me to take the time to be a team member."

Decision by Default

Teams that have a tendency to repeatedly table difficult decisions will find that their options become increasingly limited. Ironically, by hesitating, the team ultimately makes a decision—by default rather than by informed choice.

Varied Team-Member Contributions

A few members may be carrying the load for everyone else on the team. Those who are putting in the longer hours and making the greater contributions become increasingly frustrated with their "lower" contributing teammates.

Participation Gimmickry

Gimmicks to increase employee involvement and participation—like suggestion boxes—can actually have the opposite effect. When individuals are rewarded for contributing suggestions through cash payouts, there is little incentive for team members to work together to address problems and implement solutions.

Trap Savvy

Although organizations everywhere seem to be mobilizing teams, it is important to recognize that teams are not the salvation for productivity, quality, cost, and customer service woes. They are merely a tool that, when used properly, can help to boost performance. When used inappropriately, however, teams can be an invitation for disaster. Many team success stories have been widely publicized. We hear about the team at Federal Express that solved a billing problem and saved the company millions, or how a design team at Hewlett Packard cut time to market by 50 percent. What we don't hear about are the many embarrassing failures. The result? We know a great deal about what seems to make teams successful, but very little about why some teams never live up to their potential. We have only a piece of the picture—it is as if we understand why the airplane flies but know little about the conditions that could lead it to crash.

In the case studies in Part II, we will examine the most common trip wires in detail. Each case will illustrate how a team became entangled in a web of misfortune that led to declining performance. For many readers, the case studies will seem all too real and familiar. Virtually anyone who has served as a member of a team in an organizational setting has experienced at least one of these traps.

Immediately following each case will be an analysis that provides proven strategies, techniques, and tools for escaping the trap before the jaws of destruction clamp down. In Part III, we will examine how to quickly diagnose the source of a team trap so that a strategy can be developed in time to escape or bypass it. We will also come to recognize the critical disciplines that— if learned and practiced—can help to trap-proof a team.

Part II

Trapped!

Chapter 3

ᴥ ᴥ ᴥ ᴥ

The Invisible Manager

The moment of truth had come and gone for Red Houser, and he had failed the test. Deep down, he was a weary, old, autocratic dinosaur—not the new-style leader he was supposed to be. Everyone on his team disliked him right now, but, in his own defense, he had to take a stand, didn't he? What else could he have done?

Being a "coach, facilitator, and leader" wasn't his idea of management anyway. Those descriptions were just meaningless jargon coming down from on high. Some of the ideas made sense, like getting the group to coordinate the schedule and holding regular problem-solving meetings. But a lot of the other stuff—like all the talk about paradigms, redesign, and open systems—seemed way out of touch with getting a product out the door. The advice he was getting from his boss on how to manage—oops!—*lead* his team seemed equally pointless:

- "Leave the group alone, it'll do fine."
- "You've got to quit micromanaging—let the group do their own thing."
- Give 'em a direction, give 'em the authority, and then get out of their way."
- "Let them decide everything—they'll make all the right decisions."
- "Never act like an 'old-line' manager; be a coach and a facilitator."

In the heat of the bad moment he was remembering, he'd relied on his basic instincts—if the team does something stupid, you come down hard on them. Everyone learns that in Management 101. That's why Red Houser had been made a manager in the first place—he could make decisions and he could take the heat.

Was there a way he might have prevented the confrontation with his team from ever happening? After all, the group never saw him at team meetings, he was gone during most of the workday, he disappeared during lunch and breaks, and, after work, he avoided the local tavern where a lot of the team members went for a beer. Yeah, he *had* kind of vaporized into thin air—but only because he wanted to stay out of their way so they could become self-managed. In hindsight, it was obvious that management-by-vapor didn't work—the team needed coaching and training. The leader can't simply disappear and expect the team members to learn self-management all by themselves.

On Becoming Invisible

The logic behind Red's disappearing act was simple: If the manager stays out of the way, the team will perform more effectively. Often, that strategy backfires—the group flounders because it lacks direction, training, and experience. Like Red Houser, many well-intentioned managers have been victimized by a belief that if they simply abdicate their "old-line" responsibilities, improved team performance will follow. Here's how some of these managers describe the warning signs of the abdication trap.

- *The confusion factor.* "I felt confused about my role as a 'team leader.' It seemed like every day I was getting lots of mixed messages about how much control I should assert over the team. My instincts were telling me the team wasn't ready to be handed more authority and responsibility, and yet I had no idea what to do to get them ready. And there was no support from anyone else in the organization."

- *Playing the isolationist.* "I genuinely felt that my team could 'learn it on their own.' After all, this was the message my boss had been harping on for months. So I began to purposely limit the amount of time I spent with team members. The big mistake was when I started skipping team meetings."

- *The Jurassic threat.* "Some team members have accused me of being an 'old-line' manager. I was afraid my boss would come down hard on me if team members started complaining to her about my management style. So I began to tread lightly when I entered discussions. I even began censoring what I said, never exposing my concerns or my frustration with some of the decisions the team was making."

- *Initiating the unprepared.* "One day I realized: I was expecting the team to take on all this responsibility, and yet I had done nothing to prepare them. I remember thinking, 'I haven't given them any:
  —Clear direction,
  —Expectations or objectives,

—Definition of their role,

—Training in areas like meeting effectiveness, decision making, or problem solving.'

Despite a complete lack of support, I was expecting them to solve complex problems and make important decisions."

■ *The tumbleweed faux pas.* "It really struck me that I was in trouble when I began to feel and act like my opinion was far less important than those of any other team members. I found myself withdrawing and rarely making suggestions or sharing ideas. I never said anything that might be perceived as disagreement with a team member's opinion—even when I had strong concerns. I always went along with the flow."

The Point of No Escape

The point of no escape occurs when the team makes a "runaway" decision that, from a business standpoint, is unreasonable and outlandish. Like other managers before you, you may find yourself gasping as you're informed that the team has exceeded the entire fiscal year's budget in the first quarter, or the team has decided to go to a four-day workweek without consulting you. Amid the chaos, you wonder aloud, "How did this happen?"

The Vaporizing Manager

Red Houser was grumbling as he came back from the managers' meeting. The latest performance figures for his manufacturing line were disappointing—the quality figures were down, and costs were way up. He hadn't gotten chewed out by John, his boss, but that would be coming next week if things didn't start to turn around.

As he passed the main entrance of the Forest Park Circuit Board Manufacturing Plant en route back to the plating line, he noticed the sun shining through the large glass windows. He stopped for a moment and looked out at the clear blue sky, the thick green lawn of the landscaped grounds around the facility, the tall Douglas firs off in the distant forest. Nothing compared to the landscape of the Oregon countryside. He opened the door and went outside. What a beautiful day—even if his manufacturing line was going down the tubes.

He pulled a cigarette from his shirt pocket and looked across the cornfields, toward the rolling hills. He could see Mount Hood high above the panorama—a great white guardian angel overseeing the countryside below. He took a long drag.

What the hell was he going to do? Ever since the plant manager had said the words—"Our goal is for everyone to be self-managed"—the team had been sputtering; or, more precisely, he had been sputtering. His initial tack was to let the team do what it wanted—he even stopped going to the team meetings. In fact—he glanced at his watch—they were having one right now.

Wasn't that what self-management meant—let the units manage themselves? He wasn't supposed to be directing the show anymore. The group was supposed to make all decisions. "Get those closest to the work to figure out the best way to do it!" the plant manager had said. Good in theory; more like anarchy in practice. Too many people were giving orders and nobody was doing anything, except what they wanted to do. Even that would be OK if the performance was there, but the latest figures confirmed what he'd suspected from the beginning: the whole experiment was a bust. He took another long drag.

How do you regain control once you've given it up? he wondered. Probably the best thing to do was just go down there right now and tell 'em it isn't working: "I'm the manager and I need to start acting like one." Some of them would accuse him of backsliding, of becoming an "old-style" manager again. How he hated those words. Someone in the group would probably tell his boss that he wasn't allowing the team the freedom to become self-managing. That'd mean he'd get one of John's famous lectures about the virtue of teams and how self-management was part of the plant manager's long-term business strategy.

What a mess. Yeah, but he had to bite the bullet and regain control—John would pretty much leave him alone as long as the performance measures looked good. The time had come to be straight with the team—self-management just wasn't working. He was in charge, and they needed to listen to him. He inhaled deeply.

"Hey, Red, want to go for a pizza?" He quickly turned toward the employee entrance, some 25 yards from where he was standing. Scott Lewis, his lead technician, was coming out of the door. Behind him was the rest of the team.

"Huh?" he said.

"We're all going out for a pizza—we just decided to, in our team meeting. Want to come?" asked Lewis.

Red felt an explosion come across his face. The veins in his neck swelled, his breathing increased, and his heart was racing. He couldn't believe it—the stupidity, the gall! He screamed back, "You're not going anywhere! This isn't a damn country club. Get to work or else you're all fired!"

"But at our meeting today we decided we deserved an extra long break—besides, nothing critical is coming down the . . . ."

"Get back to work NOW!" His blood was pulsating at his temples. He felt his entire body tremble.

"Come on, Red, be reasonable. You know we can make these kinds of decisions. After all, we're self-managed."

That's it—John can fire me if he wants, but I can't go on like this. "Back to work, *now!* I'm sick and tired of this whole process. You're not empowered to decide *everything*. . . . That's why managers exist. So forget about self-management and listen to me for once."

Dejected, several members of the team turned and headed back toward the door. Soon, only Scott Lewis remained. He slowly walked up to Red.

"You don't know anything about empowerment, Red. You've just upset your entire team and thrown the whole effort back to zero. Way to go."

Survivor Tips

How can you avoid turning into an invisible manager? Consider the following tips.

Capability Builder

A problem often originates in how the manager perceives the best way to get results. Managers should think of themselves as responsible for the team's *development*, with a long-term goal of the team taking responsibility for its own development. If a team is given new authority and responsibility, without the corresponding knowledge necessary to use it in a responsible manner, a stick of dynamite has been lit. The following four steps are helpful in developing a team's capabilities:

1. Share all relevant business information (and make sure team members fully understand what has been presented).
2. Develop the team's problem-solving ability (through a combination of training and working directly with the team on real-life problems).
3. Develop the team's decision-making ability.
4. Ensure the team's involvement in determining the best way to get the work done. The jargon for this is "redesign." The point is simple: Work with them to come up with better ways to do the job.

The long-term goal of the manager is to get the team to a place where there is little ongoing reliance on the manager. Ironically—and this is the mistake many managers make—to create a self-managed team over the long run, managers must begin by taking an active, involved role in the short term.

The leader's role is to work with the team, help develop its ability to use information, solve problems, and make decisions. As the team demonstrates an ability to make responsible decisions, it is granted ever-increasing levels of authority, resources, information, accountability, and skill development.

Team Maturity Gauge

One tool for assessing how far a team has developed is the *team maturity gauge*. First, make a mental assessment of the experience level of the team you are working with. In your assessment, consider the extent to which the team demonstrates an ability to:

■ Take in relevant information and make decisions that have a positive effect on results.

■ Recognize how its actions impact the performance of other groups and the company as a whole.

■ Know who its customers are and demonstrate a willingness to fully meet customers' needs and desires.

■ Identify problems and implement solutions.

■ Make ongoing improvements to the work area.

■ Give constructive feedback to other team members.

■ Do each of these activities with the full participation of the entire team membership.

Teams that are unable to demonstrate these abilities are not ready to operate as fully self-directed units. Defining team limits helps to focus the team on what it can effect and prevents it from making decisions that have nothing to do with getting a product or a service to a customer.

❀❀❀❀

Based on where the team falls on the maturity gauge, define the
team's limits. Not every decision is open for debate, nor can
every penny in the budget be spent at the team's whim. The
leader must define the real limits and constraints.

One of the key changes in the managerial role during transition to a team-based work system is the shift from issuing
directives to establishing boundary conditions. Traditionally,
managers were expected to control all aspects of the way work
was performed. This level of control required issuing directives
that specified what was to be done, how it was to be accom-
plished, and who was to do it. Staff people were then expected
to execute the decisions the manager made.

In contrast, boundary conditions establish the constraints or
limitations within which the team must work. This management
technique provides the team with a higher level of autonomy
and encourages it to develop creative solutions when addressing the issues and opportunities it faces. As the team increases
in maturity and fully demonstrates the traits described on the
maturity gauge, its boundary conditions should increasingly
broaden. (See Figure 3.1 for a comparison of directives and
boundary conditions.)

Boundary conditions typically describe:

■ **Timeline:** Specifies time constraints and limitations.
  Example: Project must be completed by January.
■ **Resources:** Specifies the maximum available resources.
  Example: One contract worker will be available 40 hours per
  week.

Figure 3.1 Directives versus Boundary Conditions

Directives	Boundary Conditions
Specify what needs to be done and how it should be accomplished.	Specify the constraints and limitations that must be considered before the group determines what is to be done and how it can be accomplished.
Management-driven	*Shared leadership*
■ Provide management control over actions. Allow little opportunity for team creativity, innovation, and commitment. ■ Discourage learning while preventing blunders.	■ Provide greater team autonomy and sharper team focus. Create an atmosphere in which creative and innovative ideas are encouraged. ■ Encourage learning while preventing blunders.

33

- **Equipment:** Specifies any equipment limitations or constraints.

  Example: The project must be completed using existing computers and telecommunications equipment.

- **Authority:** Specifies the lines of command.

  Example: The team will be responsible for all process-improvement decisions. If team members feel it would be helpful to spend additional budget beyond the amount specified in the boundaries, they will need to put together a recommendation and get approval from management.

- **Philosophy:** Specifies the underlying management principles within which the team must work.

  Example: Consistent with our just-in-time manufacturing philosophy, any process improvement decisions must eliminate waste and redundancy.

- **Budget:** Specifies the maximum amount the team can spend.

  Example: The budget for this project cannot exceed $10,000.00.

- **Location/physical space:** Specifies any physical constraints or limitations.

  Example: Our offices must be housed in the 1,000 square feet of available space located in building 24.

- **Safety:** Specifies any protective constraints or limitations the team must consider.

  Example: No decisions to streamline processes can have an unfavorable impact on safety.

- **Legal/legislative:** Specifies relevant laws and/or legislation that must be followed.

  Example: All team hiring decisions must be done in a manner consistent with EEO and Affirmative Action goals.

A Rose by Any Other Name

Many efforts to create high-performing teams are needlessly stunted by the language that is used to describe the effort. A number of organizations have found the term self-management to be particularly open to misinterpretation. Among some members of the workforce, the term is interpreted as meaning: "I do what is best for me—even if that may not be what is best for the organization." If you have a choice, avoid the term self-management. It has many connotations that may raise the wrong expectations.

Naturally, using the right or wrong phrase will not, in itself, lead to disaster, but self-management is a loaded term, so why use it? "High-performance team" is a better phrase because it describes the outcome the team is attempting to achieve rather than the means to achieve it.

The Goodness Test

What do you do when the team has made a runaway decision? First, attempt to understand why the team made the decision. Conduct a kind of "goodness test." Try to remain objective, and simply ask the team: "Help me understand why this was a good business decision."

Once the team has described its rationale for the decision, calmly explain your concerns. It's important to avoid getting emotional. Stick to the facts at hand.

Then listen carefully to the response, always considering the possibility that once you understand the issue from the team's perspective, your opinion may dramatically change.

The Learning Review

A number of techniques can be used to help the team assess what has been learned from a past fumble. One method is to develop a chronology of the key events leading up to the team's mishap. By analyzing the sequence of events, team members will often unravel a series of seemingly trivial decisions that ultimately condemned the team to a significant performance hiccup.

A variation on the development of a chronology is the use of a histogram. A histogram—like a chronology—looks at the sequence of past events, but it also assesses whether each event had a positive or negative impact on team performance. Again, the power of the assessment is that it may uncover a few past actions that set the team on a course where a disaster was inevitable. Figure 3.2 is an example of a histogram.

Figure 3.2 Histogram Example

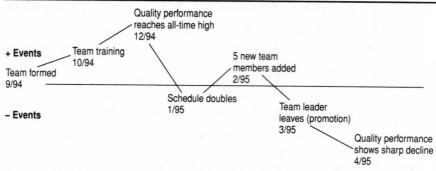

+ Events

Team formed 9/94

Team training 10/94

Quality performance reaches all-time high 12/94

5 new team members added 2/95

Schedule doubles 1/95

Team leader leaves (promotion) 3/95

Quality performance shows sharp decline 4/95

– Events

If the team has made a bad decision, sit down with the team and review the faulty approach, emphasizing what can be learned from the experience. Avoid blaming anyone or pulling rank. Just talk the team through the impact the decision has had, and let the team members explore what they learned and what actions can be taken to ensure that the mistake does not recur.

Chapter 4

※ ※ ※ ※

Team Myopia

C omplete shock was the best way to characterize Wilbur Martin's mental state. His highest performing team had pushed his company to the brink of bankruptcy—not through malice or illegal actions, but by making a perfectly reasonable business decision.

If a team comes up with an innovative idea that dramatically increases its ability to sell its products or its services, that idea is likely to be seen as beneficial not only for the team involved, but for the company as a whole. On closer examination, however, what initially appeared beneficial could be the first step toward catastrophe. As Wilbur Martin discovered, impressive team results can come at a dangerously high cost to the company.

A tendency to be too *inwardly focused* is a common team affliction. Most team members think about and discuss issues in the context of how the performance of their immediate team will improve. The impact of their decisions on the larger organization is strictly a secondary consideration. In the extreme, a kind of team myopia may develop, where the near-sighted focus of the team leads to decisions that are gravely detrimental to the business as a whole.

A single myopic team had left Wilbur Martin's truck dealership drowning in a flood of red ink. He found it incredible that the implications of what they were doing to the business were never recognized. Even now, he wondered how many members of the team fully understood how they had nearly bankrupted the business.

The Little Big Picture

Dazed, Wilbur Martin stood staring blankly at his desk. It was cluttered with reports—every damn report he could get his hands on. The more he thought about everything that had happened, the duller his stare became and the more lifeless he felt. His stomach seemed to be sinking, his mind had become a shadow. He was far too angry to show aggression, far too tired to weep. Staring at his desk—now an out-of-focus black-and-white collage of strewn papers—and trying to clear his mind was all that he cared to do. The depression was heavy, dragging him deeper.

"Wilbur." Dan Smith was coming in. Smith closed the door and looked at him carefully.

"You look like hell, Wilbur."

Wilbur focused on Smith for a moment—good employee; a little hyper at times, but well liked and trusted; a long-timer who'd worked his way up through the organization; two kids and a wonderful wife named Meg.

"How's Meg?" Wilbur asked quietly.

"What the hell? Meg? What are you talking about? She's fine, but what are you talking about? Are you all right?"

"I'm depressed." His voice seemed far away, an echo rather than his own speech.

"You have a good right to be depressed, but view this as a fluke, a one-time screwup. Nothing like this will happen again."

"Dan, don't you realize . . . doesn't anybody realize? We're on the brink, Dan. We're on the edge. It may be all over."

"What do you mean, 'over'?"

Wilbur Martin suddenly found himself very irritated. His energy came flooding back, his face felt warm. "Do you know how many truck dealerships have gone belly-up on the East Coast during this recession? Any idea? And most of them didn't do anything even remotely as stupid as we did. Get my drift, Dan? We screwed up major, and we might not be able to turn this thing around."

"Snap out of it. Sure, we screwed up and it cost us a lot of money . . . ."

"No, not 'a lot.' A lot would be $100,000, maybe $150,000. We had a $950,000 screwup. That's major league dough—hell, that's nearly 10 percent of our total sales. And, to make matters worse, we were purposely turning over customers to competitors. That damage is even greater than the horrific dollar amount. It's going to take a damn miracle to resurrect this dealership. At the very least, we'll have to lay off a dozen people. Worst case, I'll be in bankruptcy court."

"You're talking crazy now."

"Am I? I can still remember what it was like when I started this dealership 20 years ago. I risked everything I had so I could sell and service these damn trucks. My money, my car, my house— even my marriage was at risk. And I pulled it off despite some pretty damn heavy odds. This time around, I just don't know. This might be my day of reckoning . . . ."

"Wilbur, the team process essentially worked. The fundamentals are in place. We can turn this thing around."

"You know better than anyone how strongly I believed in a highly autonomous service and parts department. You went through all the team training we did. Sure, it worked—we created the finest service department and the finest parts department you'll find. But while the parts team was busy figuring out how to maximize their profit, they forgot to ask the most basic question of all—'What's best for the business?' "

❧ ❧ ❧ ❧

Les Evans couldn't believe how quickly his team had developed. He even commented to Wilbur Martin, the dealership principal, how "magical" teamwork was. "I just tell them where we need to go and then get out of their way; and 'presto,' something remarkable happens."

"Remarkable" was exactly right for what seemed to be happening over the six months since the team concept had taken hold. Part sales had skyrocketed, and inventory management had dramatically improved. Wilbur had been so impressed he'd asked Les to start sharing the team concept of management with Joe Rodriquez and several other members of his staff. He even referred to teams as "better than gold—because with them, you can make gold."

After about two months of weekly team meetings, Les had asked the team to brainstorm ideas on how to improve parts sales. The most intriguing idea came from Tommy Delgado. "We could start selling parts to other truck dealerships, particularly if they promise us a large volume of sales. They see the benefit because they won't have to carry as much parts inventory, and we'll see the benefit of increased parts sales."

Delgado's simple, straightforward idea had huge potential impact. The team quickly agreed that opening up parts sales to other dealerships would have a greater impact on parts sales than any of the other ideas they had generated. Tommy Delgado was immediately put in charge of identifying potential customers. One of the most obvious choices was Kasper International. Kasper specialized in servicing the same makes of trucks and was notorious for not having the right parts on hand.

Kasper International loved the idea. Within two weeks of Delgado's initial contact, a tentative deal was struck. Kasper International guaranteed purchase of a minimum of $250,000 a year in parts. In return, Kasper wanted a 5 percent discount on the standard interdealer pricing. Tommy took the deal back to his team and, after double-checking the figures, they reached a consensus. The deal was a go. Even with the additional discount, the increased sales volume would bring in a nice little profit. After three months, it was clear that the outside sales concept was working just as the team had envisioned.

❧ ❧ ❧ ❧

Joe Rodriquez had been around trucks all his life. His father had been an independent trucker and had taught his little "Joey" everything there was to know about trucking—from how to change a filter to how to talk on the CB. Joe's father claimed that his son knew how to pump diesel fuel before he knew how to walk.

Joe could sense things about trucks, as though he had some kind of a connection to them. Sometimes, a subtle noise—a high-pitched whining or a deep bass thump—provided the critical clue. At other times, Joe reacted to the way the mix of oil and diesel smelled or even to the pattern of the dirt buildup on the exterior of the engine.

Two days after his 16th birthday, Rodriquez joined Wilbur Martin's dealership as a mechanic. The other mechanics were skeptical about Rodriquez until they began to see him work. On

basic repairs and warranty work, he always beat the average re-
pair rate. However, his uncanny ability to diagnose problems
correctly was his most astonishing talent. Soon, every mechanic
in the shop sought him out when a particularly tough problem
seemed to defy any reasonable explanation. His ability to
quickly pinpoint exactly what was wrong and recommend a simple, straightforward fix became legendary. When Rodriquez was
21 years old, Wilbur Martin made his prodigious employee the
Service Supervisor. At age 24, the "truck shaman"—as the mechanics liked to call him—became a member of Martin's senior
staff.

Now, at age 30, Joe Rodriquez found himself the most likely
successor to Wilbur. He recognized that he was hardly ready for
that position, especially in light of the team debacle. His
biggest regret was that he hadn't confronted Les Evans, manager of the parts department, long before the sales decline in
the service group had reached such disastrous proportions. As
manager of service, he should have been aggressively looking
into why sales were tapering off, long before the bottom fell out.
But who would have thought that Les's parts team would come
up with such a crazy scheme—sell parts to a competing truck
service department at a lower cost than they would sell them to
his internal service department? That was nuts.

Joe replayed the whole chronology in his head. First, there
had been the initial grumbling from some of the mechanics in
his service department. "They never seem to have the parts we
need any more—even for basic stuff. When I tell a driver it's
going to take an extra day to get a hose, he goes ballistic, and at
8000 bucks a day out of his pocket for lost road time, who can
blame him?"

Then the grumbling started to get even stranger. "I had a guy
in here last week who was balking at the price of a filter—says
he can get it a few bucks cheaper at Kasper. I laughed at him.

'Cheaper at Kasper?' I says. 'As far as I know, they don't even have a fully staffed parts department.' He says, 'I'm tellin' ya, they're beating you on price and availability.' "

Then service sales started declining—slowly during September, then a sudden drop in October. On several days, mechanics were idle for hours—a drop in demand that he, and everyone else, had never seen before.

The real shock came when, during one of Wilbur's staff meetings, Joe casually asked Les Evans what he knew about Kasper's parts setup. Evans replied, "They basically don't have one any more. We're selling them parts . . . at a discount. It's a deal our team designed. We could offer you a similar discount if you could guarantee us the same kind of volume." Joe knew immediately what this meant, as did Wilbur, who had turned visibly red.

"Your team decided to sell parts to our fiercest competitor at a cheaper price than you sell them to our own service department?" demanded Wilbur. "Is that what this team stuff does, create brilliant decisions like that? This is unbelievable."

The following week, Guy Williams, the dealership's accountant, had a chance to unravel the whole mess. The dismal verdict came in: "According to my rough estimates, this little stroke of team brilliance will cost us about $950,000 in lost service and parts sales."

Survivor Tips

To avoid becoming a near-sighted team, consider the following tips.

Refocus the Lens

Without basic knowledge about the organization, team members will naturally have difficulty focusing their attention on the potential impact a decision could have on other teams and on the company as a whole. Simply stated, the more education team members get about the overall business, the more they will consider it when making decisions.

Ensure that team members have a base level of knowledge about the organization, its goals, and the way it is structured.

Here are some specific areas to highlight:

- Overall company or organization strategies and goals.
- Existing linkages among various departments and teams.
- Charters or missions of other teams within the organization.

Overcoming the Myopic Tendency

Recognize that there will be a natural tendency for a team to become inclusive of its own members, exclusive of others in the organization and somewhat paranoid about the intentions of outsiders. Each of these forces can potentially pull the team in the direction of increased isolation.

Given this natural tendency toward inward focus, a facilitator can help by raising two critical questions anytime the team is contemplating a decision that could potentially affect others.

1. Who *could* our decision, either directly or indirectly, affect?
2. What do you think their (those who will be affected by our decision) reaction to our decision will be? Why?

Before implementing a decision that could have a direct effect on another team or department, the decision should be reviewed and feedback from the affected group should be sought. Often, new insights will emerge that may significantly alter the original decision.

Coaching a New Perspective

If a team seems to be making decisions that are negatively impacting others, immediately provide its members with honest and direct feedback. The creators of the problem may be among the last in the organization to recognize the negative impact their creation is having.

An effective coaching approach is to describe the decision from the viewpoints of all the involved parties. This method can help demonstrate that a decision that seems like a good idea from one perspective may be a complete disaster from another vantage point. By describing the different perspectives in detail, team members will begin to develop a greater appreciation and understanding of the interdependence that exists within the organization and of the importance of taking this interdependence into consideration during the decision-making process

Chapter 5

❦ ❦ ❦ ❦

Politically Incorrect

In their zeal to make a lasting mark, some team leaders garner strength by being defiant. They challenge the validity of old assumptions and ignore the established protocol and unwritten rules of deference and respect. Although challenging the status quo is often healthy, taken to the extreme it can also carry some harsh political consequences. Dr. John Preston learned this lesson the hard way.

Despite the stellar success of his extraordinary project team, Preston became marked as a corporate outlaw, a "troublemaker." The fact that Preston didn't play by the corporate rules was not what ultimately led to his downfall—many of his harshest critics had not played by all the rules during their careers, either. No, with Preston it was his lack of grace and of acceptance of others—ironically, the same trait he so despised in the senior managers who ultimately passed judgment on his career—that led to his downfall. The point Preston never fully appreciated was that the managers who had preceded him were not stupid or irrational—they had a different perspective and worked in a different period of time. They had acted on the best information that was available and had made the best decisions they could. However, to Preston, if you weren't for him, you were against him; and being against him meant you were "old fashioned," "blind to the future," and "hanging around to pad your 401K."

Preston believed that he could ignore the political side of the organization if he simply showed results. He worked hard to build a great team, and he achieved a level of performance that most had thought was unattainable. However, in the end, his successes were overshadowed by his inability to show some humility.

A Revolutionary at Heart

Dr. John Preston stood at the podium and looked out at the audience. It was ironic that, in the front row, dressed in tuxedos, were McCarthy, Young, and DePolo—the murderer's row trio. Those three had tried every device at their disposal to kill the Pepper Project. Now they were eagerly lining up to try and get some of the credit for the project's remarkable success. Political turncoats—merely following the winds that seemed to blow in favor of their careers. No guts. Now he'd get the last laugh on them—all of them. From Wantford, the President, to Nelsen, his General Manager—they all said that the Pepper Project couldn't be done. Just a bunch of traditionalists with no imagination or vision. They had no idea what it took to create a team—a true team, where the members are so committed they'll do virtually anything, from working 90 hours a week to buying critical hardware with their personal credit cards to get around the ridiculous purchasing department. The level of commitment he was able to generate among the software and hardware engineers who made the Pepper Project happen scared the old guard.

Now he was, at long last, getting the recognition he and his team deserved. He'd let them clap a little longer before speaking. He was taking it all in. It was his moment, his turn to explain to them how managers needed to act in today's high-tech world. The clapping slowly quieted down. He let the silence hang for a moment. A little longer, then Dr. John Preston began his speech.

"Thank you for the warm ovation. It is an honor to receive the key achievement award. But let me make it very clear that this award belongs to all the members of the Pepper Project team and to those few brave souls—and it seemed a very, very few at times—who supported us in our efforts.

"When the Pepper Project team set out to create the 4900 Systems Controller, we wanted to create the best product the market had ever seen in the shortest time frame possible. That's what the Pepper Project was all about—create the best in the shortest amount of time. There's only one way you can do that here at Z-Tech: you've got to break all the rules. You've got to ignore the bureaucracy, you've got to go around the departments that get in your way, you've got to ignore requests for irrelevant information. Now all those things may seem like 'bad' behavior, but look at the results we achieved. If we had done everything by the book, we'd still be on the drawing board with the 4900. Instead, it's in the market and it's selling like mad. So, if we ruffled a few feathers, we are sorry. We had to, in order to get results; and in the end, it's results that really matter.

"Let me quickly review some of the project team's achievements:

■ The product was developed in 7 months. The previous best the corporation had achieved for the design of a product of this complexity was 18 months. The best benchmark we identified was MBI Electronics. They developed a similar product in 14 months. We beat the best by a factor of two. That's phenomenal.

■ As most of you know, we never had much of a budget for the Pepper Project. In fact, many of you in this room fought hard to keep money away from this project. Saying we did this on a shoestring isn't exaggerating. The total design budget was less than $2 million. That's pocket change around here. Our advanced engineering labs burn through a million bucks every week or so. For comparison, a similar project in the past would have cost us $5 million to $7 million to develop.

■ We had one of the smoothest transitions from design to manufacturing this company has ever seen. Why? Manufacturing technicians were part of the design team. They were directly involved in every key design decision. This product is so easy to build that one of the assemblers told me one day that his 5-year-old could build it. I said, 'Prove it.' The next day I see his son Sean snapping together a 4900 like it's a Tinker Toy set. Little Sean starts complaining to his dad, 'This is too easy. I want something else to do.' No lie.

■ Finally, we created one of the greatest teams this company has ever known. Probably the greatest team since the Z-Tech founders started building Instrument Controllers in their garage 20 years ago. To be a part of the Pepper Project was to be someone very special. Even though it's a mere six months since we completed the project, several team members have already founded the Pepper Alumni Club. We had our first get-together last month. We plan to continue the gatherings twice a year, as a way to reminisce about the project, drink beer, and get reconnected. I know of no other project in this company's history that has had such an impact on its members. I believe most of the 20 project team members would tell you that Pepper was the highlight of their professional career.

"What did I personally learn from the Pepper project? I guess it can be summarized this way:

■ First, if you're going to win in this market, you've got to challenge every sacred cow. You can't play by the old rules even if that means you have to step on a few toes. I know I wasn't always the most popular guy around here; but when the stakes are high, you've got to do whatever it takes.

■ Second, you must create a team. Pepper was successful because we had committed individuals working together as a team. There were no politics on the Pepper team, just hard work and unyielding commitment. The way you create commitment is by having every team member involved in all the critical decisions and in solving all the critical problems. The reason the Pepper Project was the professional highlight for most of its members was that, here at Z-Tech, we do a poor job of creating teams and getting people involved. That was not the case with Pepper—everybody was intimately involved in everything.

■ Finally, I learned you can be successful here even if you've got only lukewarm support. Heck, I would have actually liked lukewarm support; most of the time, it felt more like a bucket of cold water was being dumped on me. You have to forge ahead, even when the obstacles seem enormous, and keep focused on what you want to achieve. You've got to ignore the naysayers, even if they are above you in the hierarchy.

"In closing, I want to thank you for granting the Pepper Project team the prestigious key achievement award. Our hope is that what we did can be repeated many times over. Again, on behalf of the Pepper team, thank you."

Preston noticed the clapping wasn't nearly as loud now as it had been when he was introduced. The murderer's row trio were all hunched over, having a side conversation among themselves. Each of them purposely avoided eye contact with Preston as he stepped down from the podium. As he walked by Wantford, the President stood up and extended his hand. As they shook hands, Wantford pulled him close and whispered into Preston's ear, "John, you've got to learn that if you're going to be different, you must also be gracious."

❄ ❄ ❄ ❄

"Preston is amazing," said Marc Haskers, "I mean, I've worked with most of the guys on this project team before, and none of them ever committed themselves like this. You feel the energy crackle in our building."

Marla Adams, Marc's longtime girlfriend, peeked up from her fettucine and gave him her best attempt at looking interested.

"Really," she said.

"It's unbelievable," continued Haskers, "he's got this vision about how we can dominate the market in five years by drowning the competition in a 'sea of Z-Tech controllers.' He talks about the creation of an entirely new division—dedicated to an instrument controller market niche. And then there's the way he manages day-to-day—I tell you it's amazing."

"He's a Ph.D., right?"

"Yeah."

"What in? Is he a psychologist or something?"

"You would think so, the way he's got us up and running. Actually, though, he's got a doctorate in physics."

"Sounds like a brain."

"Yeah, he's a brain all right, and he's such an amazing leader."

Marla looked carefully at Marc—the round-faced, chubby software engineer she'd come to adore. It was becoming clear to her that he wanted to talk about the Pepper Project and Dr. Preston all night. He was usually quiet and reserved, but when he got excited about a topic, he would go into one of his non-stop monologues. All she would have to do was occasionally ask a question or periodically utter a "Yeah" or "I see." She really wasn't interested in Pepper—what a silly name for a project team anyway—or "Physics Brain" Preston, but Marc had a need to talk. She picked up her glass of Chianti and took a long sip. "This is going to be a two-bottle dinner with dessert and coffee for sure, if he's half as excited as I suspect," she thought. "I'll do it for Marc." She ran her slender fingers through her long, sandy-blond hair like a comb. Then she took a deep breath. Here goes . . . .

"Marc, what's new with Pepper?" She could see from his smile that monologue time was about to begin.

"I don't want to bore you." My, how polite he was becoming!

"Really, Marc, I'd love to hear." That should start the verbal flood.

"Well, to begin with, he gets us this office way off the corporate campus. The first day we move in there's the biggest pirate flag I've ever seen on the far wall, with the quotation below it: 'If you want high performance, you have to play for high stakes.' Then Preston calls a meeting of the team, stands on top of his desk, and says, 'The reason you were chosen for this project is because each one of you is running away from something—whether it was the corporate political bullshit, a half-brained manager who gave you a bad review, or the snail's pace of the company's bureaucracy. You're all outcasts on planet Z-Tech, and you've all got something to prove. I'm the biggest outcast of all,' he says, 'and I've got more to prove than anybody. This project isn't just about designing a great product; it's about proving there is a better way to design and manufacture all products at Z-Tech. We're not on a project team, we're on a mission. We're the crusaders of the 20th century out to show the corporate heathens a new paradigm.' "

"He really talks like that?" said Marla.

"Oh yeah—incredibly articulate. He's like listening to a preacher. Then he goes on about how we'll do this project in seven months, how we'll serve as the foundation of a new division, how the competition will be out of our market in three years. And what's amazing is that the more outlandish what he was saying became, the more people were starting to believe him. By the time he was through, we were all giving him an ovation."

"Yeah?" she said.

"Yeah, for real. And he has this sense—he seems to know when we need some team building or when we need to get focused back on the task. During the third month of the project, most of us were living there . . . ."

"I remember that. I didn't see you for weeks."

"Ninety hours a week was the norm—some of the guys were doing better than a hundred hours a week. We were working like crazed maniacs. In the middle of this madness, he shows up on a Wednesday at noon with a chartered bus and tells us all to get in. He's real secretive about what's up, so we're thinking he's taking us to see a demo of our competitor's machine or to see a vendor that's got something that's going to help us on the design side. Instead, we pull up to the Westgate Theater and go to an afternoon matinee of *Top Gun!* He gives us a little speech about how we're the top guns of the instrument controller world, and then we go and watch the movie. It was amazing how everybody really got into it. I mean, we're howling at the screen. After the movie's over, he says in his deepest military voice, 'If I see anybody back in the office before 0700 hours tomorrow, I'll have you court-martialed on the spot.' Tells us to go play, have some fun. Most of the guys stay at the threater and watch *Top Gun* over and over again. I saw it three times that day.

"When I got back to work the following day, there were brand new leather couches and a refrigerator filled with pop and snacks in the middle of our work area. Things kept evolving from there. Suddenly *Top Gun* baseball caps, movie posters, and models of F-14 fighter jets start showing up. One night, Williams, me, and a half-dozen other guys from the team wait until Preston has left and paint the conference room table black and put stripes down it so that it looks exactly like the deck of an aircraft carrier. The next day, Preston walks into the conference room with a customer, not knowing what we'd done. There he is looking at this replica of an aircraft carrier deck, complete with model F-14's all lined up. Without missing a beat, he turns to the customer and says, 'As you can plainly see, we're your *Top Gun* for this product.' "

Marc paused for a moment and took a sip of wine. Marla marveled at him. Part genius, part child. He was so happy with his work—he had a sense of mission and purpose, and he was having fun despite working ridiculous hours. She was envious. She wished she could be part of a team the way Marc was. She wished she could get excited while talking about work.

"What a great experience this has become for you," she said.

"Marla, I'm sure this project is going to be the highlight of my professional career."

❦ ❦ ❦ ❦

On his way out of the corporate headquarters, Preston stopped for a moment in the lobby. There, beautifully displayed, was the key achievement plaque, a picture of the Pepper Project team, and an operating 4900 Systems Controller. He marveled at it. There were only four other displays—in its twenty years of existence, the company had given only five key achievement awards. It was an incredible honor in a $1.5 billion company that came out with forty to fifty new products from its twenty-nine divisions each year.

Preston looked closely at the color picture of the project team. He looked so much younger then—the past eighteen months had really aged him. In the picture, there were no bags under his eyes, no gray hair, no permanent lines across his brow. How ironic it was that his life had gotten so difficult after Pepper's success.

He took one last look at the display—wanting to implant into his memory as much detail as he could, for future retrieval. As he turned away and headed toward the exit, he saw Marc Haskers coming in. Marc spoke first.

"Hey, John, how are you?"

"You haven't heard?" responded Preston.

"Heard what?" Marc picked up the look of concern on John Preston's face.

"The 'official version' is that I have resigned from Z-Tech . . . ."

"What? You can't be serious." Haskers was shocked.

"Unofficially, just between you and me," continued Preston, "I was forced out—fired."

"Fired?" repeated Haskers. He shook his head. He was astounded. He repeated, "Fired? The leader of the most successful product development effort in this company's history . . . fired?"

Survivor Tips

How does a manager survive the bolts of political lightning? Here are some tips.

Viva la Revolution!

Some team leaders adopt the zeal of a revolutionary as they seek to transform their team into a high-performance work system. Such enthusiasm can become contagious, putting leaders in the enviable position of having strong support from their team members. However, a potential trap can emerge. If the leader defines the source of motivation for the change in terms of destroying existing systems, processes, structures, roles, and hierarchy, it is inevitable that those who have developed and benefited from the old order are going to be resentful and frustrated, and will tend to look at the accomplishments of the revolutionary leader with resistance and skepticism. As Machiavelli observed, over 450 years ago:

> It must be remembered there is nothing more difficult to plan, more doubtful of success, nor dangerous to manage than the creation of a new system. For the initiator has the enmity of all who would profit by the preservation of the old institution and merely lukewarm defenders in those who would gain by the new one . . . . Thus it arises that on every opportunity to attack reformers, opponents do so with the zeal of partisans, the others only defend them halfheartedly.
>
> From *The Prince*, 1513

Rather than attempting to gain motivation by attacking the worth of an existing system, focus on valuing the accomplishments that the organization has made through the years. Give grace to the successes of the past while acknowledging that a new era has emerged and requires a new set of ideas and responses.

⚜ ⚜ ⚜ ⚜

By giving grace to past achievements, you are seen as building on strengths rather than attempting to tear apart weakness. There is a subtle but profound difference here. Those who have a vested interest in maintaining the status quo will pose far less resistance if you are perceived as setting a course that builds on their achievements rather than a course that challenges the validity of—and even discredits—their past decisions.

Keep the Link

In the extreme, even a team that has proven to be highly successful in getting a product to market, or providing a service to a customer, can hurt the overall effectiveness of the organization by having poor interfaces with other groups.

⚜ ⚜ ⚜ ⚜

A central part of the team leader's role is to develop effective linkages between his or her team and the rest of the organization. If the team leader, either purposely or accidentally, sends the message that the team doesn't value the opinions of others or that the rest of the organization is "backward" and "ineffective," he or she will hurt the creation of these critical linkages.

Become a Barrier Buster

Invariably, team leaders encounter organizational policies and practices that hurt their efforts to create a high-performance team. Sometimes, these barriers are subtle—such as distribution lists that limit the team's access to pertinent information. At other times, the barriers are more blatant—like having strict limits on the number of hours per month the team can be in meetings.

❀ ❀ ❀ ❀

> Team leaders must be willing to take on barriers that are hurting team performance, but they need to do so in a manner that is thoughtful and carefully planned, and that builds credibility and support within the management ranks.

The steps shown in Figure 5.1 are helpful when attempting to overcome organizational barriers. Let's examine the benefits each step offers.

1. *Recognize why the barrier exists.* What may now loom as a barrier was probably first created with the best of intentions. When taking this beginning step, it is important to understand the genesis of the policy or practice that has become a barrier for your team. The critical questions to answer are:

What was the original intent of the policy or practice?
What benefits did the company gain from the policy or practice?
In what ways is the policy or practice still useful?

The last question is particularly important—it is possible that what you perceive as a barrier has not yet outlived its usefulness to the organization as a whole. Eliminating the policy or practice may not be worth your time and effort or be in the best interest of the organization. The outcome of this step is a decision on whether to continue pursuing the elimination of the barrier.

Figure 5.1 The Path for Breaking Down Barriers

1. Recognize why the barrier exists.
2. Describe the impact the barrier is having on your team.
3. Describe how to eliminate the negative impact of the barrier.
4. Describe the potential benefits and risks of the action plan you are recommending.
5. Determine who can help you eliminate the barrier.
6. Identify opportunities to have your case heard.

2. *Describe the impact the barrier is having on your team.* Because most managers respond favorably to measurable indicators, these consequences are best described (to the extent they can be) in "bottom-line" terms. The question you are seeking to answer is:

What impact (measurable, if possible) is the barrier having on team performance?

3. *Describe how to eliminate the negative impact of the barrier.* A plan of action for getting rid of the barrier is developed in this step. The action plan should provide the specific steps that need to be taken in order to eliminate the negative consequences the barrier has created for your team. The question to consider is:

What specific changes must occur for the barrier to be eliminated?

4. *Describe the potential benefits and risks of the action plan you are recommending.* Create a realistic preview of the potential benefits and pitfalls of the change you are recommending. If risks are associated with the change, do not attempt to hide or gloss over them. Instead, affirm that you are aware of the risks, and demonstrate that you have clearly thought through ways to minimize their impact. The key questions to consider are:

What will be the benefits of eliminating the barrier?
What risks are associated with eliminating this barrier?
How can these risks be minimized?

5. *Determine who can help you eliminate the barrier.* Identify the specific individual or individuals whose support you will need to overcome the barrier. The question to answer is:

Who has the authority to eliminate the barrier?

6. *Identify opportunities to have your case heard.* Now that you have prepared your case, you must get it heard by those who have the authority to make the change happen. Having your case heard could mean setting up a formal meeting for a presentation of your ideas, or taking advantage of a "chance" encounter with an executive. The key question is:

How can I best get my case heard?

By following these steps, a team leader has a solid chance at overcoming the barriers that are holding back his or her team, without having to blatantly defy existing practices and policies. Instead of breaking the rules, the team leader becomes engaged in a constructive process of changing them.

Chapter 6

⇒⇐ ⇒⇐ ⇒⇐ ⇒⇐

Decision Paralysis

Making effective decisions is a critical skill that is often elusive and difficult for teams to master. Many common mistakes are made, and many debilitating traps are set. Some teams, in their quest to reach a consensus, fall into the trap of assuming that total agreement must occur before a consensus is reached—a difficult, if not impossible, goal. Other teams are paralyzed by the fear of making a bad decision. To such teams, it will always appear that just one more piece of information or one more meeting will be enough to finally make a smart decision. Still others see their team unravel as bitter debate over how to solve an issue splits the team into two distinct factions. Each of these ailments, invariably, leads to lengthy delays in making and executing decisions. Often, teams do not recognize that, by delaying decisive action, a *default decision* is made—and the default may be the one alternative no one thinks is reasonable.

Better Never than Late

Laura McNeil looked around the room—everyone seemed to be in agreement now. There had been a long discussion with lots of tough questions and a rigorous debate. This decision was not to be taken lightly; for it to be successful, everyone would need to support it.

"Do we have consensus?" she asked.

A silent pause. Each member seemed to be in a trance, a zombielike state. She'd seen it many times before, and it always meant one of two things: either her hunch was right and everyone was in agreement and ready to support the decision, or some members had reservations with the decision and were mentally debating the political wisdom of vocalizing their concerns. She wasn't going to let them off the hook—she let the silence continue, weighing heavily in the room. Several members of the team cast their eyes downward, staring at their tablets. She could sense their discomfort. Finally, someone spoke.

"Laura, I think we're all in agreement; let's move on." The speaker was Michael Simmons, the most senior member of the team.

"Yeah," echoed another member.

"OK," began Laura, "but before we move forward, let me restate what we've just decided and quickly go around the table, giving each of you a chance to publicly confirm your support." All eyes were on Laura now.

"The decision was to go ahead and purchase the new software from AdvantageWare at an estimated cost of $10,000. Darlene will go through the training provided by Advantage-Ware and then prepare an in-house training session so that we can be fully up and running on the program by mid-March. Is that it?"

Several heads nodded.

"Let's start with you, Monty. State your support or your reservations."

Monty, who tended to be one of the quieter group members, suddenly became animated. "I think it's a great idea. I think the AdvantageWare system is the best in its class, and Darlene, with her strong information systems experience, will do an excellent job bringing the rest of us up to speed. I say let's do it."

As Laura went around the room, asking each team member for a statement, it was clear that the team was in full agreement. After everyone had had a turn, she summarized, "We're all in agreement that we'll buy the AdvantageWare system and that Darlene will attend the training. By mid-March, we'll be fully up and running. Well done. Let's move on to the next agenda item."

The team plowed through several more agenda items, including a report on a companywide task force on waste reduction that Monica was heading up and an update from Michael on the team's performance against its key measurements. Midway through Michael's presentation, Laura noticed Suzanne coming in and taking a seat in the back. After Michael had finished, Suzanne apologized, "I'm sorry for being late, I had a customer issue to address. Where are we?"

"We're just about done, Suzanne. In fact, the last thing on our agenda is a roundtable update, and then we'll be finished." Laura smiled. The entire meeting had been very effective so far.

"I'm sorry, Laura, but I thought we were going to discuss which of the software programs we're going to purchase for the department today. I thought that was going to be on the agenda, and I think we really need to make a decision on that issue soon."

"We did, Suzanne—we're going with AdvantageWare, and Darlene is going to be responsible for the training and implementation. Everything will be in place by mid-March."

Suzanne frowned, "I'm not convinced AdvantageWare is the way to go. Did everyone see the latest review in the IS newsletter? It says that AdvantageWare has a ton of capability but runs real slow—I think speed should be a serious consideration for us."

"We already discussed that, Suzanne, and we felt the difference in speed is only a temporary problem. AdvantageWare is going to have an upgrade available within six weeks to correct it," broke in Monica.

"That's 'vapor ware' as far as I'm concerned, and I don't think we should necessarily be making decisions based on what they claim to be working on. Let's face it: all these software companies slip their schedules on products. Besides, NetSoft has a pretty good product, with a proven track record already out there. Why go with AdvantageWare when we can get it from Net-Soft? Did you know. . . ?"

"We already discussed this and reached consensus on Advan-tageWare, Suzanne. We've already decided. It's done," said Michael. He was clearly irritated.

"Don't you think you should do a thorough job of investigat-ing options, particularly cheaper options, given the budget con-straints we're currently facing? NetSoft's product lists for a couple grand less."

"It doesn't do what we need it to—you'd know that if you'd been here on time and heard all the discussion. We already de-cided as a team. The decision has been made," said Michael, his voice rising.

"Huh, I thought I was a member of this team. Just because I have a more diverse view doesn't make me wrong, does it? I thought we were supposed to respect diversity of thought. I think we need to look at some additional facts. Besides, a mid-March implementation is completely unrealistic—I couldn't send any of my people to training then. I'm not convinced Darlene is the right one to do the training."

"Are you purposely trying to tear apart everything we just decided?" broke in Michael, his face now flushed.

"Maybe Suzanne has a point," said Monica. "I mean, I did feel a little rushed. Maybe we should revisit this at our next meeting."

"Yeah, I for one feel violated by the decision the team has hastily reached. There is a lot more information we should be looking at," said Suzanne.

"We're running out of time," said Laura. "What do you want to do?"

"I guess we'd better revisit the decision at next week's meeting," said Monty. "It sounds like Suzanne really needs to be involved in this decision and she doesn't feel good about it."

"OK. Anyone else have any suggestions?" There was silence. As Laura looked around the room, she could see Michael shaking his head in frustration.

"Well, let's revisit the decision on which software to purchase at our next meeting then. Because you brought up the issue, Suzanne, can you plan to come prepared with an alternative proposal?"

"Actually, next week won't work for me. I'll be out of town," said Suzanne as she looked at her appointment book. "Could we set up a special meeting tomorrow?"

"It's going to be impossible to get us all together tomorrow," responded Michael.

"I don't know what to tell you—I've got all kinds of customer meetings over the next couple of weeks. Besides tomorrow, the soonest I could meet would be in about three weeks. It's either tomorrow or in three weeks."

"Show of hands: who can meet sometime tomorrow?" asked Laura. Only Suzanne and Monty raised their hands.

"How about Saturday?" said Suzanne. "I mean, this seems pretty important and people need to show their commitment . . . ."

"Why didn't you show your commitment by getting to this meeting on time?" said Michael. His voice was cracking.

"Hey, I was with a customer. They are the ones who pay the freight. It's either Saturday or three weeks out. Which is it?"

"Can't we do something over e-mail?" broke in Monica.

"This is ridiculous!" said Michael, standing up. "See you in three weeks. I've got another meeting to go to."

"Me too," said Suzanne. "Laura, could you make this a topic for the team meeting three weeks out?"

"You know, I don't think we'll be able to get Darlene into the AdvantageWare class if we don't make a decision inside three weeks," noted Monica.

Michael and Suzanne were gone, off to separate meetings. Laura looked around the table at Monty, Monica, Karen, and Caesar—who'd been uncharacteristically quiet. Now he spoke, "What a mess. What a terrible mess." Everyone nodded.

Survivor Tips

How do managers avoid the consensus trap? Consider the following strategies.

The Electric Consensus Acid Test

A common question when forming a team is: "How will we make decisions?" Depending on the nature of the situation facing the team, some decision-making methodologies work better than others. In circumstances where immediate action must be taken (e.g., a medical emergency or the evacuation of a burning building), a highly autocratic approach, with one individual taking charge, is usually the most effective. In such instances, immediate action, without any deliberations, is critical to ensure the safety and well-being of others. Conversely, it would be considered an outrage if a judge, rather than a jury, decided the guilt or innocence of a defendant in a criminal trial. In this instance, utilizing a jury of the defendant's peers helps ensure that the evidence is more fairly considered.

Generally, the situations faced by teams are neither emergencies requiring split-second response nor issues needing days of deliberation and unanimous consent. In fact, the most effective decision-making method for the majority of issues facing teams is consensus. Figure 6.1 describes the advantages and disadvantages of various decision-making methods.

Consensus is often misunderstood. Some view it as being the same as unanimity, meaning that everyone on the team thinks the best possible decision has been reached. Others view consensus as more like democratic decision making, where the

Figure 6.1 Decision-Making Matrix

Method	Examples	Advantages	Disadvantages
Autocratic	A task force submits a proposal to a division head and waits for a final decision. A manager decides on the work schedule and then informs the group.	Effective for making decisions quickly. Most useful in emergencies where immediate action is critical. Works best where clear lines of authority are established.	Although decisions can be made quickly, actual support and implementation of the decisions may suffer. As the complexity increases, the quality of autocratic decisions decreases because fewer perspectives are considered.
Democratic	A nation elects a new president. Union members vote to accept a new labor agreement. Team members vote to elect a team leader.	Allows a large number of people to voice their preference on issues. Ensures that the majority wins. Decisions can be made relatively quickly and efficiently by simply calling a vote.	In small groups, voting tends to encourage people to take sides. This rivalry can impede both the quality and the implementation of a decision.

Consensus	A work crew agrees to support new process changes. A team establishes a set of operating guidelines.	Ensures that there is open debate of all issues and ideas and that every team member has a chance to provide input. Complex decisions are well thought out, resulting in high-quality decisions. All team members support the decision once it is made.	The consensus process can be relatively long and challenging. Reaching consensus requires a great deal of communication, patience, and understanding of others' views. Effective facilitation is necessary to ensure that all team members have the opportunity to voice their opinion and share their insights.
Unanimous	A jury deliberates a court case and renders a unanimous verdict.	Ensures that everyone on the team thinks that the best possible decision has been made and will openly support it. Dissension and conflict are minimized.	Because no two people think exactly the same, reaching a unanimous decision may take an extremely long time. In the work setting, unanimous decisions often cannot be made.

issue is ultimately decided based on a vote of the team's members. Consensus is neither of these. The following description is very helpful in defining consensus:

> Consensus does not mean that everyone on the team thinks the best possible decision has been reached. It does mean that no one is professionally violated by the decision and that all team members will support its implementation.

Having a clear, concise definition of what consensus means is terribly important. By defining the term, people can recognize whether they can agree with the decision or whether there is a need for more discussion and analysis.

Two acid tests are inherent in this description. The first test is: "Am I, as a member of this team, professionally violated by this decision?" If my answer is "yes," then I am obligated to state my dissent to my team. If my answer is "no," I move on to the second acid test. The question each team member now must ask is: "Will I actively support the implementation of this decision?" If my answer is "no," again I am obligated to explain why I cannot support the decision. If my response is "yes," then I have agreed with the decision. When each member of the team has either explicitly or implicitly stated "no" to the first acid test and "yes" to the second, the team has reached consensus.

Even for an experienced team, reaching consensus can, at times, be a difficult and time-consuming process. Reaching consensus requires a willingness, among all team members, to listen with the intent to understand the positions of others and to willingly engage in a dialogue that allows numerous alternatives to be openly considered. Having a clear description of what consensus does (and does not) mean is an important first step in improving team decision-making effectiveness.

Navigating toward Consensus

When facilitating a team toward a consensus decision, there are four important guidelines to remember:

1. *Clearly define the issue facing the team.* Common sense says that a good decision cannot be made if the issue being discussed has not been clearly defined. Too often, teams jump to developing solutions without first recognizing the real nature of the issue. In the extreme, the team may develop an elegant solution that does nothing to address the real problem.

2. *Focus on similarities between positions.* Rather than focusing on differences of viewpoints and opinions—a natural tendency when the team seems split and clear factions are forming— focus on the similarities that exist. Be sure to point out the areas of commonality and agreement that exist between the two sides. Amplifying those points on which there already is general agreement helps move the group forward.

3. *Ensure that there is adequate time for discussion.* All team members must feel that they have had ample opportunity to state their case. Decisions that are perceived as being "railroaded through" weaken the entire team—participants begin to feel that it really does not matter what they think or say. To ensure that each person has had a chance to have his or her position heard, it is helpful for the facilitator to individually ask each member of the team how he or she stands on the topic and whether he or she has any additional comments to make.

4. *Avoid conflict-reducing tendencies (e.g., voting).* If a team gets stuck and feels that it cannot reach a consensus, it is natural for team members to want to resolve the impasse by taking a vote and going with whatever the majority decides. This tendency can set a bad precedent. If the team quickly resorts to voting each time it has difficulty reaching

consensus, then it loses all the benefits that consensus offers (e.g., open sharing of diverse viewpoints and strong
support among all team members when implementing the
decision). Generally, it is a far better strategy to let the
group continue to struggle with the issue and explore new
alternatives until consensus can be reached.

When facilitating a meeting where the team is attempting to
reach a consensus, remember these guidelines: (1) clearly define the issue facing the team, (2) focus on similarities between
positions, (3) ensure that there is adequate time for discussion,
and (4) avoid conflict-reducing tendencies (e.g., voting).

Norm the Destructor

If a team doesn't have a clear and established set of ground
rules, a set of accepted practices or "group norms" will evolve
over time. Some of these "norms" can prove counterproductive.
In some team settings, for example, it is acceptable to interrupt
others during a discussion or to arrive at a meeting late and
challenge decisions that have already been made.

Teams need to consciously choose the ground rules by which
they want to operate. These ground rules should define such
things as how meetings are best conducted, how decisions are
most effectively made, how leadership can be shared within the
group, and how feedback is given to team members in a constructive manner.

Ground rules are the essential architecture for ensuring effective meetings and team interactions. Ground rules provide a common vision of how the team should act, and they help create a sense of ownership among team members in regulating the behaviors of the group. Some specific examples of ground rules include:

■ Meetings start and end on time.
■ Only one person speaks at a time.
■ Decisions are made by the consensus of the team.
■ The agenda goes out prior to the meeting.
■ If a team member expects to be tardy or absent from a meeting, he or she is responsible for getting his or her position, on any issues that will be discussed, presented by a team member who will be attending.
■ All team members are responsible for keeping the meeting focused and on track.

The entire membership of the team should be involved in developing the ground rules. In this way, all members "buy into" the rules of conduct, and each member is far more likely to support them on an ongoing basis. A simple process to follow in developing ground rules is:

1. Provide some examples of ground rules and how the team can use them to improve the effectiveness of team meetings and other forms of team interactions.
2. As a team, brainstorm a list of possible ground rules. (In brainstorming this list, try to think of ground rules that would help address issues that have hurt team interactions in the past.)
3. Review the brainstorm list and come up with a final list of 5 to 10 ground rules.

4. Have the finalized list printed out and posted in the room where the team most regularly meets.

5. Refer to the list during meetings, to help keep the team on track. At the end of each meeting, review the list and briefly discuss how effective the team was at upholding the ground rules.

6. Periodically review the ground rules and make changes or improvements to them as necessary.

Meeting on the PATIO

Sending out an agenda in advance transfers a large amount of the responsibility for the meeting from the facilitator to the meeting participants. When they can see the agenda before the meeting, participants are aware of what they must be prepared to discuss. The agenda should also give participants the approximate time during the meeting when each topic will be under discussion.

In developing an agenda, use the PATIO process. PATIO is an acronym standing for Purpose, Agenda, Time, Information, and Outcomes. Each of these elements helps create a well-structured meeting agenda.

■ *Purpose.* When preparing for a meeting, the first step is to define the primary purpose of the session. Is the meeting, for example, to share information on a critical issue or to resolve a problem facing the team? The purpose statement clarifies the primary reason for the meeting.

■ *Agenda.* The agenda lists the issues that will be covered during the meeting.

■ *Time.* The approximate time allotted to each agenda item should be described to project an estimated total time for the meeting.

Figure 6.2 A PATIO Meeting Agenda

Purpose:

1. Receive feedback on revised project outline.
2. Review action plans and assignment status.

Agenda:

1. Review each section of the revised project plan outline.
   a. Record feedback on the whiteboard.

Outcome: *A complete list of feedback from all team members.*
The feedback will be reviewed by the planning subteam and used in developing version 2—final version—of the project outline.

2. Review action plan.

Outcome: *Review of the status of all current action items. Identification of any dates that are in jeopardy of slipping.*

3. Roundtable.

Outcome: *Information updates, presented by each team member.*

4. Review of meeting effectiveness.

Outcome: *Identification of ways to increase the effectiveness of the meeting.*

Time:

■ Date: September 21
■ Duration: 8:00 A.M.–10:00 A.M. (2 hours)
■ Location: Lake Michigan Conference Room, Building 78

Information:

■ Review project plan (revision 1) prior to the meeting. Bring your copy.
■ Action plan sheet will be handed out.

- *Information.* Attendees should be told about any information that should be gathered or any prework that might be necessary prior to the meeting, and/or any handouts that they will receive during the meeting.
- *Outcomes.* The anticipated outcome (e.g., share information, solve a problem, or make a decision) of each agenda item should be described.

Figure 6.2 is an example of a meeting agenda prepared using the PATIO process.

The effectiveness of a meeting is largely determined before the participants enter the conference room—the key is in the planning. Poorly planned meetings inevitably lead to poor results. Meetings designed using the PATIO process will be more efficient and effective. Further, getting the agenda out to participants in advance can go a long way toward eliminating frustrations related to unprepared or late participants.

Chapter 7

❧❧❧❧

Brain Wars

Behind the scenes in corporate America, a fierce war is being waged. The weapons are computers, databases, and telecommunications devices. At stake is the dominance of the high-tech industry.

In the information age, the intellectual and creative potential of a company's workforce is the gateway to competitive advantage. As a result, the strategies and tactics for gaining the best and brightest have become increasingly sophisticated. Headhunters scour the latest breaking news, looking for hints of dissatisfaction within a company. Once possibilities are identified, they quickly tap into powerful databases, call up their networks, and search reports and journals, piecing together vital information. Within a few hours of a restructuring announcement, numerous top performers have been identified and contacted, and interviews have been arranged.

A seemingly harmless cut to shore up profits can quickly turn into a draconian nightmare. One mistake, and even the best managed companies may find themselves victims of electronic raiders.

Picking Your Brains

Carol Sato was starting to feel the wear and tear of the 60-plus-hour workweeks. Her neck was stiff, her shoulders were tense, and she was feeling edgy. As she logged on to her computer, she could feel her eyes straining—the screen was even starting to look a little blurry.

"Phosphorous Eyes" was the nickname her ex-boyfriend had given her. He had never fully understood her job. The few times he had come to her workplace, she had always seemed to be at the computer screen, scanning resumes, checking news updates, reading e-mail from her colleagues, or tapping into one of the hundreds of databases she could access in a search for the perfect candidate to fill a job. He had never understood that head-hunting wasn't a "nine-to-five" kind of job. Hunters had to be there when the prospective candidates could take calls—especially when the prospects were executives and senior-level professionals from other companies. A certain etiquette had to be followed. Prospects were never to be called at work until they gave you permission to do so—and most never did. So, by necessity, many of Carol's phone calls were made in the evenings and on weekends. And, of course, there were dinner meetings she had to go to, and stints as a sight-seeing guide. Sometimes, she even had to act as a real estate agent—trying to convince prospects that they could get a house just as big, and send their kids to a school just as good, if only they'd come to LogicTek. She had to give and give and give during her long workdays.

When she got home, what she needed was support. That's where everything fell apart with Tom. He was as needy as a prima donna software engineer.

The cuckoo clock on the wall just behind her in the eight-by-eight office was singing away. She suddenly became aware of the time. "Damn, it's eight o'clock," she mumbled at the persistent bird. Having been in meetings or candidate interviews all day, she hadn't had a chance to look at her e-mail. The window on her screen announced that she had 157 unread messages, at least a third of which required some kind of response. She did a rough calculation in her head—a minimum of two more hours' at work. "Ah well, it's not like I need to rush home for any reason," she lamented.

The first 40 messages were run-of-the-mill updates and commentary. A new product had been released in the consumer division, a new senior manager had been hired in the Database Group, the founder was pleased with the first-quarter results, a new procedure was being discussed for getting screened resumes into the database more quickly. And, of course, there was some horsing around—Martin was still trying to sell his car to "anyone foolish enough to buy it," Anne's date with Jay had been a dream, and Hansen had concocted a piece called "Educational Devolution," in which he lampooned math education over the past 30 years.

As Carol continued to scroll down through the messages, she could feel the emptiness in her stomach—hunger pains. She hadn't had a chance to eat anything since breakfast. Without lifting her eyes from the monitor, she reached into her desk drawer and fumbled around for her secret stash of fat-free granola bars. Eyes still forward, unwaveringly fixed on the brightly glowing screen, she tore the wrapper with her teeth and started chomping. A faint hint of strawberry was encased in sawdust, but it would do for now.

She read and deleted another dozen or so messages. The next one to pop up on her screen was titled URGENT. She read on:

carolsa:

here's the deal—this is a real mind blower and huge—i mean mega, Goliath, KING KONG kinda HUGE—

Underland, inc. is in troubel with a das kapital T. we've had a hell of a time recruiting from these numskulls in the past because all the developers and senior types considered underland heaven on earth. great benefits, good pay, and an emphasis on teamwork. hell, one guy I tried ot recruit said he'd be letting down his team if he split— oh please give me a break and pass the kleenex!

well those dayz are over, gone, finis. the prez has lost his bandwidth and gone stupid big time so here's our chance to gain some primo people. while they're not using the L word (lay-offs, of course) they are "selectively encouraging poeple to leave." comp has been rduced by $153 mo. on avg, they've taken several top developers out of win-dow offices and stuck them in cubicles, and linked compensation to the market performance of the projects a developer is working on. in fact, you can lose as much as 25% of your base pay if a project bombs. considering the fact underland couldn't market rolling paper at a Grateful Dead concert, I don't see to many developers anxious to work on new products and to make matters worse their existing dbase offerings aren't exactly kicking butt. i don't see any developers looking to the future with any anticipation. the team stuff is gone, empowerment has become a bygone word, the spirit is broken. bet that guy i tried to get would gladly give up a redundant body part to join us now. the mood at underland is grim.

here's my favorite quote, "we'd be ok if the prez would keep his mouth shut. everytime he opens his mouth our stock drops." gotta love him. (you're probably wondering how I founda ll this out—i'd tell you but then i'd haveto kill you.)

hope this brightened up your day as much as it did mine. recruiting from these guys is going to be like pickin dandy lions from a vacant lot. EAZY :) :) :) :)

see ya'

lannyda

She'd heard rumors about the problems at Underland but not in this detail. The news was very surprising. Underland was renowned for being a great place to work. The company had always stressed teamwork and had developed some phenomenal products. All of that appeared to be going by the wayside, if Lanny was right. Carol had seen this pattern before: loyal employees who would never have considered leaving their company were doing a complete about-face now that downsizing, comp cuts, and nutty pay schemes had entered into the picture. If Lanny's source was accurate, there would almost certainly be some top talent to pluck away.

Carol took another bite of her granola bar and then grabbed her mouse. With a couple of clicks, she was deep into a database, ready to run a search.

Search by? COMPANY. Click.

All matching sources? YES. Click.

Company name? UNDERLAND. Click.

Survivor Tips

To survive the brain wars, consider the following tips:

Don't Clear-cut

If you scour the research, you'll find that downsizing, rightsizing, delayering, compressing—or whatever your personal euphemism is for removing people—usually doesn't work. Most of the companies that were involved in the downsizing binge of the early 1990s lived to regret their actions. More than 50 percent of all downsizing efforts failed to result in improved organizational performance over the long haul. If your organization is fat and bloated, effectively manage attrition (i.e., don't replace employees who retire or leave the company), offer buyouts, or cut back on work hours. Avoid going in with an ax.

❀ ❀ ❀ ❀

> The data are very clear—don't cut to shore up the quarter's profits or to impress stockholders. Only cut when you have no other reasonable choice—when, quite literally, the survival of the business is hanging in the balance.

Reorganization Dialogue

A good rule of thumb to consider during a reorganization is: If you lose one great employee, it's very disappointing, but there's a chance the organization will be able to recover; if you lose two top performers, their leaving is devastating to the organization as a whole; and if you lose three, you have an outright disaster on your hands and have probably seen only the tip of the iceberg—chances are that many others will soon be leaving. This formula applies whether you have a 40-person department or a 500-person division. Many managers don't think of the potential consequences of a reorganization in those terms, but losing a single high performer is a huge potential setback.

Make sure everyone is aware of what's happening every step of the way. The worst-case scenario occurs when people are surprised by the reorganization and unclear about how they fit into the new structure. People will naturally assume the worst of intentions on management's part—regardless of what management's real intentions were. Without communication and dialogue, frustration and turnover prevail rather than understanding and support.

> The key to a successful reorganization in troubled times is communication and dialogue. Communicate why changes must be made, and engage in a dialogue in which alternatives can be openly explored with the people who will be directly affected by the change.

The Morale Advantage

High morale is critical for effective service and customer responsiveness. If there is a high level of dissatisfaction in an organization, don't expect employees to keep it all inside and provide great customer service. The simple fact is that employees tend to treat customers with the same level of respect, understanding, and responsiveness they are receiving from the organization. For this very reason, a number of companies have aggressively begun to measure employee morale (through surveys and focus groups) and to hold managers accountable for improving the morale in the organizations that they manage.

❄❄❄❄

Think of morale as a competitive advantage that is as important to maintain as state-of-the-art technology, superior customer service, total quality, or rapid time to market.

High morale is not gained by employee-of-the-month plaques, suggestion boxes, or free dinner certificates. Rather, high morale is a complex combination of factors, including:

- Degree of freedom on the job.
- Clarity of work role.
- Sense of stability and security.
- Free flow of information and open communication.
- Fair pay and benefits.
- Sense of rapport and teamship.
- Regular performance feedback.
- Knowing the "big picture," including the company's strategies, financial performance, and long-term goals.
- Meaningful work.
- Training and development opportunities.
- Ability to balance personal and work life.
- A sense of trust and mutual respect between managers and nonmanagers.

A morale advantage can be created by focusing energy on developing each of these critical factors.

Chapter 8

❧❧ ❧❧ ❧❧ ❧❧

Transition Blues

A temporary leader creates a trap that can ruin even the best laid plans. The importance of leadership in creating a high-performing organization is well documented and widely accepted. What's often forgotten, however, is the need for this leader, whoever he or she may be, to stick around for a while. When a strong leader serves as a catalyst for change but then isn't around to see the change through, his or her efforts will likely have little lasting impact on the organization. In story after story, a similar conclusion can be drawn: leadership continuity is a critical consideration.

The warning signs that trouble could be lurking in the wings include:

■ *The Frankenstein effect.* A sudden, unexpected change in the leadership of an organization can send nearly everyone scurrying for cover. Will the replacement espouse the same management philosophy? Will he or she believe as strongly in the team approach? If the team is still in its relative infancy (less than two years old), the loss of the leader can have disastrous consequences, especially if his or her replacement has an entirely different approach and philosophy. As one employee described it, "How do you keep the momentum when the leadership style shifts from Jimmy Stewart to Dr. Frankenstein?"

■ *Successionless planning.* Succession planning is a critical tool for ensuring smooth management transition. Most organizations don't have good (or *any*, for that matter) succession planning in place. In the worst-case scenarios, the "Peter Principle" prevails: an individual moves upward in the management hierarchy until his or her highest level of incompetence has been reached. Poor planning can lead to putting managers into positions that they are simply not prepared to take on.

What happens when there is a dramatic change in leadership within a team-based organization? David Healy feared the worst and wanted to be prepared for it.

The Shadow Knows

The Saab 900 felt tight as it cruised down Chuckanut Drive— the windy, twisty stretch of road perched high above Puget Sound between the city of Bellingham and the rural community of Burlington. David Healy downshifted as he went into a sharp curve. As he came out of the curve into a short, straight stretch of road, he gazed out at the gray of the Sound and the distant black-green of the San Juan Islands.

Healy loved driving the Chuckanut route—the constant hum of the car and the rhythmic movements of the shifting, breaking, and steering allowed him to clear his mind of the sales branch clutter. He entered a Zenlike trance, his mind keenly aware of the physical beauty that surrounded him. He savored the sky-ward-reaching firs with their large round trunks, the bright red of the leaves on the ancient maples, the ghost gray of Puget Sound, and the threatening white of the overcast sky. If he weren't running so late, he'd stop at one of the wayside over-looks and take it all in for a few minutes. Perhaps on the way home—yes, on the way home.

Healy noticed a landmark he'd remembered from an earlier trip—a four-foot-diameter stump from a fir tree logged a good half-century ago. It was on the edge of the road, just off the shoulder. He knew he was less than a kilometer away from the Oyster Creek Inn. Undoubtedly, Stevens would already be there, notebook in hand and a serious expression on his face. Stevens was a good consultant, and Healy needed some good advice. It was a shame how things were about to change—especially after so much time and energy had been put into getting the organization to operate like a tightly coordinated team.

Healy could still remember how restless and dissatisfied he'd become before Kevin Royer arrived as the new branch manager for the Vancouver, British Columbia, sales branch of International Computer Systems (ICS) back in 1990. Royer was an unlikely combination of youth and wisdom, aggressiveness and patience. He seemed unconcerned with company politics; yet he was the most effective manipulator of the company's political system that Healy had ever seen. It was as if Royer knew he'd beat the ICS system by politely defying it. Even people who should have been Royer's harshest critics marveled at the seemingly effortless way he managed. No matter how difficult or serious the discussion, or how risky and intense the decision, Royer always appeared to be having fun, and his enthusiasm was contagious.

The mountains of bureaucracy and the nonsensical reporting structures—coupled with the Canada-wide recession—had put enormous pressures on the branch prior to Royer's arrival. Revenue had to go up in 1991—way up. The chances of the branch getting additional resources were nil; in fact, it was clear that anyone who left the organization would not be replaced. Healy could remember thinking that Royer was about to get eaten alive because everything was running against him at the branch. Yet Royer, with his boyish optimism and polite manner, seemed undaunted. Just being near him instilled tremendous confidence. Healy had racked his brain trying to figure out what made Royer tick. The way Royer got people's commitment was the damnedest thing.

Part of Royer's success was embedded in the way he chose to manage the organization. He introduced a variety of practices that were virtually unheard of in other parts of ICS. For example, he was enthusiastic about what he called "high-performance teams" and how they could be applied within the branch. He had even sought Healy's advice on how to develop a process that would involve the entire branch in designing a new organization based on team concepts. Royer then sent Healy and two other members of the branch to the United States for some additional training. Healy had met John Stevens during that training time.

Armed with what he had learned from the training, and with a voracious appetite for books on the subject of teams, Healy found himself becoming a kind of expert. His knowledge was quickly recognized by Royer, who started to use him as his personal consultant. Royer regularly solicited Healy's advice on process and design issues. Healy took on the responsibility for conducting skills training for all the members of the newly formed teams. He worked on revamping the organization's measurements and headed a task force that completely re-worked the way performance reviews were handled. Healy was having the best time of his career, and the results were stunning. The number of managers had shrunk from eight to two through a combination of attrition and reassignments. The revenue and profitability of the branch had dramatically increased, customer satisfaction had skyrocketed, and morale was at its all-time high. A reorganization that dismantled the functional departments and created a new structure where teams were aligned with specific customers had been successfully implemented with virtually no disruptions to the branch.

However, everything appeared to be changing now. Healy hoped that Stevens would know what to do and what to look out for. Whenever Healy or Royer felt stumped with an organizational issue, they'd call Stevens. In fact, Healy had met with Stevens a half-dozen times over the past several months, usually at the Oyster Creek Inn—a kind of midpoint between Stevens's Seattle office and Healy's office in Vancouver. Stevens called them "shadow" meetings because actual decisions were rarely made. Rather, the focus was on designing processes that the teams could use to resolve issues on their own.

"We should not be telling the teams what to do," Stevens once noted. "Rather, we should help them define processes so they can quickly and effectively determine their own courses of action."

Healy parked his car and rushed into the quaint restaurant. Stevens was sitting at the corner table. His open notebook was spread across his place setting, and a half-finished beer stood in front of him. He was looking out the window at a glistening waterfall in the ravine directly below the restaurant.

"Hello, John."

"David, how are you?"

Healy blurted it out. "Royer's been promoted. He's leaving Vancouver for Toronto within a month."

Stevens returned his gaze to the waterfall below. "So he didn't take my advice."

Healy was surprised. He had no idea Royer had already discussed the promotion with Stevens.

"When did you talk to Royer about the promotion?"

"I haven't; I had no idea he'd been promoted. I will have to call him and give him both warm congratulations and a harsh scolding."

"What did you mean when you said 'He didn't take my advice' then?"

"Toward the end of my very first meeting with him, I told him he needed to make a two-year commitment to this project or run the risk it would all be for naught. My second piece of advice was that if he did have to leave because of an opportunity he simply could not refuse, he needed to make sure he had a say in who his replacement was."

"I'm afraid he's 0-for-2 then. The guy who's slated to replace him is a tyrant—a friend of mine works for him now. My friend is relieved, I'm nervous. Very nervous."

"You're right to be nervous. The Vancouver branch is in a very delicate state right now. . . ." Stevens stopped and took a deep swallow of beer. He put down the glass and gave an ironic grin, "If Royer hadn't been so damn good, the branch wouldn't be in this mess now."

⛄ ⛄ ⛄ ⛄

Applause filled the auditorium as Kevin Royer finished his presentation. They had been so attentive, carefully hanging on his words. The questions were good, and his story was a good one too. He felt he'd been completely honest about the success and downfall of the Vancouver branch without pointing any fingers or making accusations. Yes, it had gone well.

It was odd, thought Royer, how the interest in the Vancouver story lingered on and on. Nearly three years had passed since he'd set foot in the glass, steel, and concrete tower in the heart of Vancouver, British Columbia; yet, that was the story he had been asked to tell at the company's first symposium on team-based work systems. Something about the Vancouver effort captured people's imagination. The perfect success and the perfect failure were combined in a single story. A classic example of the profound achievements high-performing teams can make was also a lesson in how fragile the team structure is.

In hindsight, he wished he could have taken the advice Stevens had given him shortly after he became the manager of the Vancouver branch—"Make it a two-year commitment," he'd been told. But the promotion was just too good: more responsibility, more pay, and the chance to get back to his hometown of Toronto, where most of his family and friends remained. So, less than two years after heading west, he found himself on an Air Canada flight returning east.

Shortly after his departure, things started to deteriorate fast in the Vancouver branch. The new branch manager found the team structure an interesting idea but felt it lacked enough individual accountability. After all, where were the individual revenue targets under this system? What was to keep a salesperson from being a "slacker"? Individual quotas were soon resurrected—breaking apart the team measurements Royer had been instrumental in establishing. A level of management was soon added to "keep an eye on the teams and ensure that decisions are made more quickly." A reorganization followed; the old functional organization was reestablished. Several key employees left, and performance started to slip. Within 18 months, the organization was consolidated with another branch and only a fraction of the employees who were there under Royer still remained.

Royer knew most people blamed his replacement for the decline and downfall of the Vancouver branch, but Royer knew better. He too had played a role, and that fact bothered him a great deal.

Survivor Tips

How do you avoid the leaderless trap? Consider the following tips.

Wasteland Detour

In many companies, regular transfer of managers is still a common practice. In fact, a transfer is often a sign that one's career is still on the rise. Although the diversity of experience a manager can gain from these transfers can be a great benefit, there are also numerous negative consequences that are often overlooked. The lack of leadership continuity, particularly in a developing organization, can set everything back to zero.

A second problem is that transferring managers promotes short-term thinking. Imagine you're a fast-track manager and you know the typical pattern is a one-year assignment followed by a transfer. That pattern means you've got 12 months to prove you're a shaker and baker. What's the easiest way to get impressive results in a short time frame? Cut out training and development; minimize nonproduction time; get nasty about attendance, tardiness, breaks, and vacations; don't spend any money on capitalization; and keep costs to a minimum. Squeeze, squeeze, squeeze until the turnip is bleeding. When the year is up, in all likelihood, you'll get promoted because the numbers look good. What is left behind is an organizational wasteland. Turnover skyrockets and the competitive position slips.

Two to four years between moves goes a long way toward achieving long-term perspective and a high degree of leadership continuity while still ensuring that managers get a diverse experience base.

❦ ❦ ❦ ❦

The point is: Make sure a long-term perspective can be maintained and a high degree of leadership continuity is in place.

Cultural Fit

Typically, the only consideration when making a change is whether the new leader has the necessary technical knowledge. Technical expertise is often important, but the fit of the newcomer's management philosophy and style with the needs of the organization should be an even greater consideration. This matchup is especially relevant in team-based organizations—so much so, that "fit" should be the *key* consideration. Some of the critical questions to consider are:

■ What has been his or her experience with teams?
■ What is his or her backup style? What are his or her tendencies in high-stress situations?
■ How skilled is he or she at coaching and facilitating groups?
■ How does he or she respond to ambiguous situations?

An effective strategy to ensure that a new manager will be a good fit with the organization is to have the team he or she will be managing conduct the hiring interview and make the final hiring decision. By being directly involved, the team can define the qualifications it considers essential in the manager, and can test, through the interviewing process, which candidates have those qualifications.

When making a leadership change in an organization, determine whether the new manager is going to be a good fit with the team culture.

Chapter 9

⁓⁓⁓⁓

Hesitating the Team Away

n an age when organizations must make and execute decisions quickly in order to stay competitive, the slightest delay
can have enormous consequences. Nowhere is this need for
quick execution more obvious than in design teams that are
working at tremendous speed and under a great deal of pressure to bring new products to market before their competition.
Chase Friesen was just beginning to see the impact that decision-making delays could have on his team and the company's
business. The potential for disaster was very real, and he suddenly found himself unsure of what to do.

In an ideal world, team members would be equal contributors
and get an equal say in team discussions, but, in reality, there
are usually personalities who dominate, and Chase's team was
no exception. The dominant personality on Chase's team

seemed bent on messing up everything. He seemed only to care about his agenda, regardless of what would be best for the team. And he kept challenging the consensus of the team, creating delay after delay on several key decisions.

As the team leader, Chase was embarrassed by his own hesitance to confront the problem team member. He could tell that everyone else on the project was waiting for him to say or do something. Chase felt awful about his inaction, but he also felt trapped by circumstances—the problem employee was a brilliant design engineer, and the team desperately needed his ability. And, to make matters worse, he was well known and well liked by the company's executives. He wasn't the kind of person Chase wanted to upset.

So Chase hesitated, choosing to do nothing and hoping—desperately hoping—that things would somehow work out.

Hamlet's Flaw

"We've got to do something . . . we're always stuck. It's like we know too much." Chase's comment was followed by silence. The summation had struck a chord with several people on the team. They *did* seem to know too much—every decision was painfully scrutinized, every angle was voiced, and piles of documentation were reviewed before anyone dared venture an opinion. Then, after hours of debate, a compromise was usually reached that no one cared for or really supported.

Melanie broke the silence, "We've got to take a hard look at how we operate as a team, if we're ever going to meet our schedule. We're already two months behind our critical-path target dates, and the way we're slothing along, this thing could end up a year or more behind schedule."

"And we know, from that meeting last week, top management says every month we delay costs over a million bucks in lost revenue," added Smith.

"I think the actual figure was closer to $800,000," broke in Carla.

"It completely depends on the competition and how fast they move. Could be $800,000 a month if nothing much happens; could be one, two, or even three million if Simpson Controls comes out with a comparable system—which we believe they are working on. The bottom line here is that we've got to get moving or else this project is toast," said Chase Friesen, the team leader of the Thunder project. He continued, "I think Melanie is right: We've got to take a hard look at how we're currently operating, if there is any hope we're going to steer this back on track. The problem—and the solution—are in this room."

"Chase, what you said earlier, that we know too much . . . I think you were onto something. I don't think it's that we know too much; it's that we spend so much time sifting through reams of information to get the one or two key kernels. I'm a perfect example. I came to this meeting 15 minutes late today because I spent over two-and-a-half hours sifting through e-mail. One day's worth of e-mail, 176 messages. I'm on every distribution list there is. So what did I learn today? In the 176 messages, there were three I would consider relevant to the Thunder project team," said Melanie.

"Let me capture some of these ideas on the whiteboard." Chase stood up, quickly grabbed a pen, and started writing.

■ Too much e-mail.

"I think the problem is that the information is too haphazard and unfocused. We don't know what we do know, if that makes any sense," said Smith.

"Strange," thought Chase, "it seems to make perfect sense." He wrote a second item on the board.

■ Information lacks focus, too random.

"We take as much time, energy, and analysis dealing with a trivial, relatively inconsequential issue as we do with an important one. Regardless of how small the mole hill is, we'll make it into a mountain," noted Smith.

"Let's face it, we've got bad meeting habits. There's rarely an agenda, people are late, people interrupt when someone else is speaking, there's little facilitation and—I hate to say this as I look around and see the level of experience, knowledge, and expertise in this room—but we need a heavy-handed facilitator. When we get into these meetings, we often act more like third-graders than professionals," added Carla.

"I've taught third-graders," broke in Melanie, with a smile. "They are much easier than this group."

Chase added another fault to the list.

■ We need more discipline in our meetings.

"Despite the fact that we're all supposedly 'great' project managers, I think our project management skills stink," began Melanie. "Every one of us—and I'm maybe the worst offender— has made a verbal commitment at one of our meetings that he or she knew full well couldn't be met. We've got to get realistic and honest about our own limitations here, or else we'll get into this vicious cycle of delay after delay."

Chase, who had been busily writing down all of the items on the board, took advantage of the momentary pause. "Is there anything we do well?" he asked, trying to lighten the conversation up.

"No," said Sanders viciously, "absolutely, positively nothing. We're the number-one company in our industry because we're a bunch of no-good numbskulls who don't know anything about how to design products. Come on, get real. Sure, we've made some mistakes, but this is not an easy project. Management knew from day one that a 12-month development cycle would be unrealistic. If we came in 6 months behind schedule, they'd be amazed—there isn't some awful, 'You're killing the business' pressure here. Overall, we're doing OK despite some technical hiccups we could have never *ever* have anticipated. My own feeling is that we can waste a whole lot more time watching Chase write down our gripes, or we can get back to our agenda and solve some real problems. All this talk we're doing now isn't getting us one minute closer to our completion date."

A long silence followed Sanders's outburst. Chase looked at Sanders, unsure of what to say or do. He knew most of the people in the room thought Sanders was a big part of the problem: he was always among the first to tear apart an idea—and, boy, was he good at it! Sanders was exceptionally bright (he had received his first patent just before his 16th birthday and had pulled a 780 out of 800 on the math section of his high school SAT). However, he always seemed bent on showing off how smart he was, and that rubbed a lot of people the wrong way. Chase knew no one had ever confronted Sanders about his attitude—they were afraid of the verbal assault they'd receive as a rebuttal.

Smith sat motionless in the silence; he had seen this classic pattern before: Start down one path to improve the group process, only to see it stopped before it went anywhere. What did it matter anyway—he'd be gone before Thunder ever got to market. Only last week, he'd been contacted through a headhunter by a firm located in Oregon. He'd always wanted to fish the Pacific Northwest; now he'd have the chance. He imagined himself with a brand new rod, paid for with his signing bonus, on the bank of the Rogue River in southern Oregon. He could almost feel the rhythm of the cast and the sound of the fly as it whisked above his head and then dropped effortlessly, without so much as a ripple, into a big pool just behind a large boulder.

Melanie, who had at one time idolized Sanders, now looked at him with disdain. He was pompous and arrogant. He always acted as if he knew more than anyone else about how to manage a design team. He was one of the "untouchables" because of his legendary achievements—but his last big success was over five years ago. Five years was an eternity in high tech. How she wanted to confront him, to let him know how out of line she felt he was and how his attitude was hurting the team. She'd seen him, on more than one occasion, verbally assault several of the younger engineers for what he considered "piss poor" design work. She couldn't get herself to tell him how angry he made her feel—the risk was just too great. She'd told Chase, and from the conversation it was clear he felt the same way. Chase wasn't going to do anything, though, because even as the team leader he was scared of Sanders. Sanders was the type who'd hold a grudge and become an even bigger pain or, worse, he'd go up the management chain and get you taken out. He had that kind of clout with the senior group—he could get people in a lot of trouble.

Carla wished Chase would start acting more like a leader and quit caving in to Sanders. Sanders seemed to run everything—his opinion always carried double the weight of everyone else's. The fact was, he was a rotten manager! He was disorganized, he rarely communicated (except when he was angry about something), and he was a loner. The best place for Sanders was by himself in a fully equipped lab somewhere offsite, where he'd never come into contact with anyone from the company. When he came up with one of his brilliant technical ideas, he could beam it back to headquarters. That was the only way Sanders was going to benefit the company anymore: isolate him. On a team, he was a completely destructive force. And Chase just let him run amok. Sanders was killing the project and there was nothing she could do. Every day, when she came to work the nightmare just recurred.

"So what do we do now?" asked Chase.

"Why don't you start by erasing that psychobabble from the whiteboard and getting us refocused on the technical issues we've got. I haven't seen a single hybrid chip yet, Smith. What the hell is going on?" said Sanders.

The trout fantasy would have to wait. "Didn't you get my e-mail—sent it last week," responded Smith.

"You know I never bother with e-mail. If you've got something important, personally hand it to me. I don't have time to look at all those damn messages—I just delete them unless they're from the president. Hey, there's a solution to your problem, Melanie—just push 'delete all' whenever your mail stacks up." Sanders let out a chuckle, then continued, "So what's the deal with the hybrid, Tom?"

"This seems way out of line with what we were just discussing. Don't we have some ground rules here, Chase?" said Carla.

"Yeah, well, ah . . . what should we do now?" asked Chase again. His face was flushed and hot, not from anger but from embarrassment.

❈ ❈ ❈ ❈

Over dinner, Chase explained his frustrations relating to Sanders and the entire Thunder project to his wife, Susan. She listened attentively as he described how Sanders had disrupted that day's meeting—just as he had disrupted many previous meetings. Finally, she asked, "And what did you do?"

"That's just it, Suz, I did nothing. It's the same with everyone else on the team—they do nothing as well. Everything just stays the same and we experience it over and over again."

"Hesitation will end in tragedy, you know. Just like Hamlet." Susan was an English teacher at the local high school. She often brought in literary examples that Chase, being from an engineering background, had been surprised to find oddly helpful.

"Help me out here, Suz. What's a thousand-year-old Dane got to do with this?"

"Hamlet's tragic flaw was his inability to take decisive action. At every opportunity to avenge the wrongful death of his father, he hesitates. What he fails to realize is that each time he hesitates, he is becoming more engulfed in a tragic web of events. From what you've said, it seems to me you've got Hamlet's flaw. Each time you fail to confront the issue, you may be fueling the Thunder project's tragic demise."

Chase thought for a moment about what she had said and then smiled. "I never did care much for Hamlet—all the actors talk so funny."

Despite his joking, Susan could tell the message had sunk in. She, too, smiled.

Survivor Tips

To avoid Hamlet's tragic flaw, consider the following tips.

Dangerous Default

An important point to bring to the team's attention when it is having difficulty making a decision is the impact of not deciding anything. Remarkably, some groups will delay a critical decision for so long that ultimately their inaction leaves them with no possible alternatives—in effect, the decision has been made by default.

A good question to pose when the team appears completely deadlocked is: "What are the consequences of not making a decision today?" or "What will be the default if we aren't able to decide?" Often, the consequences of not making any decision are more grave than those of some form of action.

Disaster Avoidance

Choosing to avoid giving feedback to a disruptive team member will almost never improve the situation. In most instances, the opposite will occur: The negative impact of the problem will tend to increase, the longer it is left unaddressed. The cumulative effect of not addressing the problem directly will be seen in the intensifying frustration of team members and in an overall decline in their work performance.

When a team member is disruptive or performing poorly, his or her actions may be the result of a lack of knowledge and training, a misunderstanding, unclear priorities, a poor job fit, or personal issues that have nothing to do with the workplace. Rarely is someone purposely destructive and difficult, but without an opportunity for a two-way dialogue, the complexities of the issue will never be known and the best course of action will remain unclear. Further, the person receiving the feedback typically does not recognize how his or her behavior is disruptive to others, just as the person giving the feedback often does not understand the factors that are contributing to the observed negative behaviors.

In general, feedback should be given immediately after the negative behavior has been observed. The exception to this guideline is that feedback *should not* be given at a time when it would be publicly humiliating to the individual receiving it. In most cases, feedback to correct a negative behavior should be given in a private, one-on-one setting. Remember, the goal of providing feedback is to encourage open dialogue that results in positive action—the goal is *not* to punish the person for what he or she did.

Feedback needs to be nonjudgmental in content, and it must focus on the observed behavior and the impact it had on the person or persons who observed it. When giving feedback, do not guess as to the effect the behavior had on others—talk specifically from your own experience. "I" statements are very helpful. "When I observed you *(description of the behavior)* I felt *(description of the impact it had on you personally)*."

The five basic steps in giving effective feedback are:

1. *Observe the behavior.* When appropriate, provide feedback immediately after an observed negative behavior.

2. *Give the feedback.* Focus on what you personally observed and the impact it had on you.

3. *Listen to the other perspective.* After giving your feedback, listen carefully to the recipient's point of view.

4. *Develop an action plan.* Work together to define what (if any) action needs to be taken as a result of the feedback meeting.

5. *Review progress.* If appropriate, agree to a follow-up meeting to see how much progress has been made toward achieving the action plan you jointly developed.

A Political Life

All organizations have an inherent level of political activity. Some of this activity is healthy (e.g., debating strategic direction, and lobbying for and reviewing new product concepts) and some forms of organizational politics are destructive (e.g., abuses of power that employees find threatening).

Often, the perceived political threat is far greater than the real political threat. People rarely get fired for coming up with ideas that will improve the performance of the business.

If you are going to take a stance that may appear to be politically unacceptable, keep focused on what is in the best interest of the business—even if your stance may ultimately cause some grumbling among the management hierarchy. Always convey your message calmly, in matter-of-fact terms, to convey that you are not interested in political gain, only in business performance. And, perhaps most important of all, *take action.* By hesitating, you are damaging your personal integrity.

Ironically, most executives do not want their organization to be made up of followers who are great at taking and executing orders—they want people, working in teams, who can independently identify opportunities or issues and take immediate action. The stereotype of the executive seeking compliance from his or her employees is an outdated and inaccurate portrait. Enlightened executives want action.

Everyone as Coach

Having team leaders who are skilled at giving feedback is important, but one of the benefits of going to a team-based design is that each team member can give feedback to every other team member. This important interaction is often overlooked.

❦ ❦ ❦ ❦

> In high-performance teams, giving constructive feedback that helps to *correct* negative behaviors, *develop* new capabilities, and *reinforce* desired actions is the role of all team members.

Having all team members capable of giving feedback does not give team leaders or managers an excuse to merely wait until someone on the team handles a difficult situation. Saying that feedback is everyone's responsibility means just that—everyone. Further, members of the team will be looking to the team leader to set an example. If he or she models a lack of feedback skills or is perceived as being intimidated, others on the team are less likely to step forward. The more the right kinds of behaviors are modeled, the more they will be adopted by others on the team.

Dealing with Disruptions

Keeping a team focused and on track during a meeting is not an easy task. Any team, regardless of its sophistication or maturity, may fall prey to disruptions, digressions, or other

nonconstructive activities. At the point when the disruption begins to affect the team's ability to solve a problem or to make a
decision, it is time for an intervention.

❀ ❀ ❀ ❀

> Ideally, once a disruption has occurred, all team members
> would be equally capable of getting the team refocused and
> the meeting back on track. This, in fact, should be a long-term
> goal—creating a team fully capable of self-regulation. Most
> teams, however, rely on the meeting facilitator to take the lead
> in dealing with the problems that arise. For this reason, the fa-
> cilitator must have some strategies for dealing with the disrup-
> tions he or she is likely to encounter.

A facilitator can implement an array of antidisruption strategies.

■ *Model effectiveness.* For a team to be effective, a high degree of
rapport and trust must exist between the meeting facilitator
and the team members. The facilitator can build this rapport
by modeling effective techniques when giving feedback and
when asking others to provide feedback in return. If the facilitator is trusted by the team members, they will be very
attentive when he or she does intervene to deal with a disruption.

■ *Be patient.* Peer-to-peer feedback will often have a more profound effect than feedback from a manager or a designated
meeting facilitator. So, when a disruption occurs, wait to see
whether another team member will address it.

■ *Be preventive.* Well-planned and well-prepared meetings—
those with a clearly defined agenda and posted ground
rules—are less likely to be disrupted. Take the extra time
needed for adequate preparation.

■ *Observe the process.* Pay attention to the meetings "hows"—how issues are being discussed, how decisions are being made, how problems are being solved, and how much participation is actually occurring. By observing the group process, the source of the disruption will become apparent. Share your observations with the team and work jointly with them to identify ways to improve the manner in which the team functions.

■ *Name the disruption.* Often, this strategy involves little more than stating the obvious. Using nonjudgmental language, describe the disruptive behavior after it has occurred. For example:

> "I believe we are off-topic now."
>
> "I don't believe your comment is relevant to our current discussion."
>
> "I feel as if this is a digression."

■ *Use the ground rules.* Refer to the ground rules as a way to remind the team of its agreements about how meetings should function.

■ *Share responsibility for meeting success.* During the course of the meeting, ask questions such as:

> "How do you feel this meeting is going?"
>
> "What could we do to improve this meeting?"
>
> "Does everyone feel there has been an opportunity to express an opinion on this issue?"

By asking well-timed questions, you begin sharing the facilitation role by inviting group members to provide their observations and inputs.

■ *Appreciate differences.* The strength of the team structure is in the diversity of its membership. By having a variety of opinions, ideas, and skills, the team is better poised to make good decisions and build on each other's strengths. Remind members that differences of opinion are natural and healthy.

Chapter 10

᠅ ᠅ ᠅ ᠅

A Box of Trouble

"Quick and easy" is a seductive phrase—especially to managers who are see their work hours spiraling upward and the complexity of their jobs increasing. So, when information began to seep out of Japan that suggestion boxes were a key ingredient in Toyota's remarkable quality performance, North American managers were eager to adopt the idea. After all, a suggestion box was cheap (paper, a box, an evaluation committee, and a little cash for payouts were all that was needed), could be quickly implemented (no change in any existing systems, structures, or roles was required), was virtually risk-free (no damage control was needed if it failed), and created a sense of involvement and participation among workers. The suggestion box appeared to be a truly "quick and easy" fix.

Not surprisingly, the suggestion box craze of the 1980s resulted in little widespread improvement. The very factors that made it quick and easy also made it ineffective. If management philosophy, systems, and processes don't change, then widespread participation and involvement weren't—as company after company learned—likely to occur.

As they realized that getting true participation and involvement was neither quick nor easy, many organizations began focusing on changing the way they fundamentally operated. This change meant top-down support, formation of teams, widespread transfer of information, increase in meetings and training, wider availability of resources, and delegation of authority for decisions to those actually performing the work. As these changes began occurring, the suggestion box became a tired and seemingly harmless relic of the past. What many companies failed to recognize was that in the new, team-based workplace, the suggestion box was anything but harmless. The suggestion box was, in fact, an idea killer.

The Idea Killer

With only 10 minutes left until the next final assembly team meeting, Meryl Livingston was, much to her surprise, excited about getting together with her team. The team had met on a weekly basis for over two months and was starting to work well together. Meryl, like most of the other assemblers, had initially been skeptical about the meetings—management always seemed to be trying some new fad. Programs flew around the plant like sparrows in the springtime countryside. In the past three years, initiatives in total quality, just-in-time, reengineering, and a suggestion program called "idea mania" had been tried. Ninety percent of these programs were a waste of company time and money. So, when the high-performance teams were announced at the quarterly plantwide meeting, Meryl had been politely skeptical.

The first two meetings of her group had consisted of basic training on how to operate as a team. Meryl learned how to hold an effective meeting, how to set up team ground rules, how to reach consensus, and how to use a step-by-step process for solving team problems. She and her coworkers had been impressed. Already, the team was applying what it had learned. In fact, at the most recent meeting, the discussion had focused on how to streamline the manufacturing process, and some excellent ideas had emerged—particularly from Phyllis Johnson.

Phyllis, the oldest member of the team, had been with the company only 18 months. Her husband, Vincent, had retired from IBM with a generous early retirement package when he was 55. After his retirement, he and Phyllis had traveled extensively across the United States and Canada. On their frequent trips, they would visit their three children and seven grandchildren, who all had ended up on the West Coast, far away from their hometown of Burlington, Vermont.

Vincent loved retirement and pursued his numerous hobbies—golf, fishing, and woodworking—with passion. Oddly, the more Vincent seemed to enjoy the fruits of retirement, the more Phyllis recognized that there was something missing for her. At 61, having not held a job outside the home since her marriage to Vincent some forty years earlier, Phyllis decided it was time for a change. She typed up a resume, bought a new dress, and, with Vincent's wholehearted although somewhat surprised support, begin interviewing for jobs.

When Phyllis was offered a job in final assembly at Williams Industries, she was ecstatic. The work was not easy for Phyllis: it required significant finger dexterity, a lot of getting up and down from her workstation, and a considerable amount of walking. Occasionally, she had painful flare-ups of arthritis in her right hand and knee. However, she always managed to get her work done without a complaint. In just a few weeks, she had mastered all the skills necessary to do the entire final assembly sequence. In the process, she had also become popular with the other members of her team. Phyllis was a gifted conversationalist and an equally astute listener. People loved to hear her engaging, often hilarious, stories.

At the last team meeting, Phyllis had suggested a series of changes that she believed would make the entire final assembly operation more efficient. Her ideas ranged from rearranging the setup of the workstations (so that tools would be more accessible) to having parts delivered directly to the workstations rather than to the central storage area. As Carl, the recorder for the meeting, wrote the list up on the whiteboard, Meryl Livingston smiled. "Phyllis, if we did all that, we'd save this company a bundle. How did you ever come up with these ideas?"

"It's the darn arthritis—it gets my brain thinking about all kinds of ways to do things more easily. It only makes sense that if I can come up with a way to make it easier for me, there's a good chance that the idea might make it easier for all of us."

Because of the Labor Day holiday, two weeks had passed since the last team meeting. The agenda, which was always sent out the day before the meeting, was entirely dedicated to reviewing Phyllis's suggestions and then coming up with an action plan for getting them implemented. Meryl took out her team binder and reviewed the notes from the last meeting. Wow, did Phyllis ever have some good ideas!

"Meryl, you're not going to believe this—this guy is a real jerk." Meryl looked up. It was Tino Franchez, another member of the assembly team.

"What are you talking about, Tino?" asked Meryl.

"The company newsletter was just delivered so I grabbed a copy, and what should I see on the front page but this . . . ." Tino handed Meryl a copy of *BizWeek*, the company's weekly newsletter. He was pointing to the lead article.

Idea Maniac Randy Sommers Wins $500!

Have a good idea? Randy Sommers, a Final Assembly Associate in Building 34, did, and he got $500 for it, thanks to Idea Maniac—the company's suggestion box program!

Sommers figured out a way to make it easier for employees in final assembly to share common tools by rearranging the work area into a U-shape. This approach will mean less nonproductive time for employees and fewer tool purchases for the company. A big cost savings! Randy wrote up his innovative idea and submitted it to one of the Idea Maniac suggestion boxes.

According to Human Resources Director Anne Stevens, "This is exactly the kind of ideas we're looking for—the ones with bottom-line impact. When we got Randy's suggestion, we immediately did a cost–benefit analysis and estimated that his idea will save the company over $50,000 a year once it's implemented in all of our final assembly areas. That's a tremendous cost savings!"

General Manager Bim Miles noted, "Participation in the Idea Maniac suggestion system hasn't been as high as we would like, but when people see that a good idea means good money, I suspect the ideas will come flooding in."

If you have a good idea, simply fill out one of the Idea Maniac cards found next to the suggestion box. And remember, good ideas mean good money!

"Wait a second, that was Phyllis's idea, not Randy's—and we were going to work on it as a team. What is he trying to pull?" said Meryl.

"Oh, I think it's pretty obvious what he's trying to pull—the jerk. He takes Phyllis's idea, writes it up nice and pretty, and then runs off with $500—what a jerk. And you know what's worse—I bet nobody shares any idea with anyone else from here on out. I mean, why? So some mindless creep can get paid for stealing it?"

Survivor Tips

To avoid a suggestion box nightmare, consider the following tips:

Owning the Solution

To achieve high performance, teams must be empowered to identify problems, make recommendations, come up with practical solutions, and take ownership for implementation. In contrast, suggestion systems are based on the premise that management will receive ideas, evaluate their merit, and then determine whether they will be implemented. In a suggestion box system, the idea is generated by an individual who—in all likelihood—will never have to implement the suggestion that he or she has submitted. The suggestion box is merely a way to share ideas, not a way to create a sense of ownership for results.

Submitting suggestions is important, but the ultimate goal of a high-performance team is to implement solutions. Ironically,

---

As a general guideline, any suggestion box system already in existence should be discontinued during the transition to a team-based workplace. The odds are that the continued use of the suggestion box will serve to stunt the development of the team as an effective improvement-generating unit, particularly if recognition and rewards for suggestions are given only to individuals. In the extreme, idea stealing may occur, with one individual getting a payout for another team member's idea. This misuse of team ideas perpetuates a sense of distrust among members of the team and reduces their willingness to openly share their ideas.

suggestion systems can actually hurt the development of teams that are attempting to take on the increased responsibility of correcting problems or implementing improvements. Figure 10.1 shows the problem-solving hierarchy.

Money for Nothing

A recent study on the effects that monetary rewards have on improving academic performance among children yielded some noteworthy results. The group of children who were told they would receive money for solving a particular problem had, on average, poorer performance, tended to be less interested in the task, and showed less creativity than the control group, who were not offered any enticement to solve the same problem.

Figure 10.1   Hierarchy of Problem Solving

High Involvement

Ownership
Team is directly responsible for all aspects of problem solving and implementation of solutions (i.e., problem identification, recommendations of alternative solutions, and responsibility for ensuring that the problem is "designed out" of the process). The team addresses problems relating to the performance of their work as well as competitive, organizational, and customer-related issues.

Resolution
Team is directly responsible for identifying and implementing solutions to problems encountered in their work area.

Recommendations
Team makes recommendations to management for possible solutions relating to problems encountered in their work area.

Identification
Team is asked to identify problems in their work area. Any solutions that are developed or any actions taken are solely the responsibility of management.

Low Involvement

The children who were given the incentive tended to do the minimum amount of work required to receive the money. Once the money was received, they quit the activity and showed no continued interest in it. In contrast, long after the initial puzzle was solved, the control group continued to work on problems they had not even been assigned. The difference in the results of the two groups was so profound that researchers concluded that the monetary reward seemed to actually work against the children's developing any interest in the activity or applying what had been learned from it. In short, the monetary incentive detracted from learning.

Although the study focused on children, the same tendency can be observed in adults—monetary incentives do not necessarily create a desire to solve problems or to share improvement ideas. In fact, the emphasis on monetary rewards as part of a suggestion system may actually create a scenario that parallels what occurred among the students: employees contribute only the minimum required to receive the cash payout. The result to the company is mediocre, often poorly thought-out suggestions.

Cash payouts in suggestion systems are based on an outdated perspective of what motivates people—money, alone, does not motivate. In fact, intrinsic factors—having a say in how to perform the job, having autonomy in choosing a schedule, being directly involved in making decisions and solving problems, and receiving feedback about performance—will create far higher levels of personal motivation than a small cash payout.

Chapter 11

~~~~~~~~~~

Tyrannosaurus Team

"High commitment" is a phrase reserved to describe only the most devoted and focused teams. On such teams, members have been known to bring in their sleeping bags and catch brief naps as they worked through the night to solve a nagging quality problem; or, they have flown back early from vacation to help another team member close a critical deal. On a more sinister note, some high-commitment teams have been known to engage in "midnight acquisitions," "borrowing" vital tools from neighboring departments or breaching the company's computer security protocol in order to access confidential information that the team decides it needs to know.

Although high commitment is a desirable goal for any team, teams can cross the line into an unhealthy state of obsession. Such teams can ultimately become analogous to a Tyrannosaurus: a creature of great size and strength, with a headstrong disposition and a tendency to devour anything that's in its path.

Devour the Leader

John Iverson was known as the "brilliant slob"—a nickname he personally took great satisfaction in having. He was a legend within the organization. His technical expertise was considered second to none, and his Jimmy Stewart-like personality made him universally popular. John's desk was equally famous—piled with stacks of papers, reports, books, sticky notes, memos, a half-dozen coffee cups (several partially filled with coffee from the previous week), half-eaten sandwiches, plastic trays from the cafeteria, a pile of empty soda cans, a computer with little notes taped all around the edge of the monitor, and a mouse pad with a giant coffee stain that looked like an ink blot from a Rorschach test.

Despite an outward appearance of clutter and disorder, as exemplified by his office, John Iverson was actually an extremely organized and disciplined individual. His staff meetings were generally acknowledged as highly effective, his follow-up on action items was tenacious, and he would provide detailed responses to e-mail, faxes, or phone messages within minutes of receiving them. He spent the first half-hour of every morning mapping out what he wanted to achieve for the day, and in the last half hour of the evening, would evaluate how effective he had been.

When Iverson was named vice president of operations, he'd been both excited and overwhelmed. Operations had always been on the bottom of the corporate pile in terms of equipment, budget, and training. The predictable results were poor quality, flat output, and rotten morale. Within a week of being named VP, Iverson doubled the training budget, signed off on several hundred thousand dollars' worth of capital improvement, and formed a design team to develop a plan to transform the operations group into a high-performance organization.

The design team's work produced an organization aligned around products and key customers rather than functions. Under the new structure, the 500-person organization was configured into 50 natural work teams. Each team had a designated team leader—typically, the former supervisor. The team leaders were initially responsible for setting up the team, facilitating its meetings, interfacing with other teams, and communicating upward to management.

The combination of the new structure, the increase in training, and the improved equipment yielded immediate improvements. Within the first six months, production increased 20 percent, quality improved nearly 10 percent, and the latest employee survey put morale at an all-time high. The "brilliant slob" was getting accolades from the company president as well as persistent phone calls from outside organizations hoping to tour his facility for benchmarking purposes. Everything was going better than he could have possibly hoped.

But now this—Iverson still couldn't believe what he was hearing.

"Let me make sure I'm hearing you right. You want to kick your team leader off the team?" Iverson repeated, saying each word very slowly and deliberately to the five employees from the medical products assembly team who were sitting around his desk.

"Yeah, that's it exactly, John. He's not helping us; in fact, he's hurting our team. I mean, Mel's a nice guy and all that, but we'd do just as well without him. He's deadwood. Besides, it seems to us that's where this team stuff needs to go anyway—we don't need managers anymore. We're self-managing," said Clarence Talbot, who was acting as spokesperson for the five.

"What did Mel say when you told him all this?" asked Iverson, still in disbelief.

"We sort of told him indirectly last week. We locked him out of our team meeting. He was late, so we locked the door and wouldn't let him in. It turned out to be the best meeting we ever had."

Iverson's jaw dropped. "You locked your team leader out of your meeting?"

"Hey, he was late. He knows the rules. We start on time. You know how important that is—I hear your meetings always start on time too, John. We're just like you."

"Except I never lock people out," replied Iverson.

"Oughta try it; they'll never be late a second time."

John Iverson looked across his desk at the five employees. They had a fierce intensity. He could remember saying, during one of the plantwide meetings that he held each month, that anyone was welcome in his office at any time. Although he had said the words, no assemblers had ever taken him up on it— until now. He had to admire their courage. He knew that talking to a vice president was a big deal to them. He guessed that, until he had come on board, they probably didn't even know who the vice president of operations was, let alone what he looked like.

"You know," continued Talbot, "Mel's situation isn't anything like what we did to McCormick."

"Sam McCormick? I know Sam. I don't remember hearing anything about Sam," said Iverson.

"Mel probably never told you—he was furious when he heard what we did. You see, we all felt McCormick wasn't pulling his weight . . . ."

"He wasn't; he was a slacker," confirmed a dark-haired member of the group whom Iverson didn't recognize.

"McCormick was clearly slacking off, see?" continued Talbot. "He was coming to work late, taking long breaks, going home early, and his performance numbers were terrible, so the team took a vote. The next day, McCormick finds his lunch pail on the steps of the employee entrance with a note attached, 'Shape up or you're out,' followed by every team member's signature. I'll tell ya', he hasn't stepped out of line once since then."

Iverson was speechless. What had he created? Although he admired their commitment, they were starting to take the team concept a little too far. He decided to redirect the conversation.

"As I recall, the performance of your team has been pretty good," he said.

"Best among all the final assembly teams of all product groups. We've had perfect quality for two straight months, productivity is up 43 percent, no unplanned absenteeism, cost is down by 22 percent, and we keep our area spit-shined and polished—you could use a little of that here, if you don't mind me saying so." Talbot's eyes were fixated on Iverson's overflowing garbage can.

The youngest member of the group, a 19-year-old with sandy blond hair and a scraggly mustache, broke in, "We're good, really good. And we enjoy being a team and planning out how we're going to get the work done. It's awesome. Did you know we never stop working until we've made our goal for the day? Last week, when the test line was down, every one of us put in a 20-hour day, took a 4-hour nap, and then got going again. There ain't no team like ours."

"Don't you think Mel had something to do with getting you guys up and running?" responded Iverson. "Wouldn't you agree that Mel's role as team leader has been critical to the success you've had so far?"

"Don't get us wrong—we like Mel. And yeah, he helped in the beginning. This isn't about his performance or anything—I mean he works hard and all that. We just don't need a team leader anymore. It's really as simple as that. We don't need him. We can manage ourselves. We do better when we manage ourselves."

As Iverson looked toward the five of them, they all nodded in unison, as if the scene had been choreographed.

Iverson persisted, "Don't you see that Mel has direct access to information and resources that you guys need? He helps keep you running like a well-oiled machine. He needs to be there; he has a valuable role to play . . . ."

"John, it was scary coming in here—none of us wanted to do it, but we felt we had a good idea and you'd hear us out. We were hoping you'd help us—after all you are the 'team guy' around here and the only decent VP this company has ever had. We all appreciate the way you manage this organization—you're straight with us. But it's looking like, where the rubber really meets the road, you're not going to give us your support. We don't need a manager anymore. We don't need one and we don't want one. As far as we're concerned, having Mel there just hurts our chances at getting a bonus. If you want to really help make self-managed teams work, you'll let us run without him."

The last thing Iverson wanted was to be perceived as not supportive. "I haven't made a decision yet. I need to talk to Mel before I take any action—surely you understand that. I have to admit I'm a little taken aback by what you've said. I guess I just didn't expect this."

The blond man broke in, "We're good. We're gonna be the best self-managed team you've ever seen. Nothing is going to stop us!"

❀ ❀ ❀ ❀

"Well, John, what do you want me to do?" Mel looked horrible. There were enormous rings under his eyes from his sleepless night. His hands were visibly shaking, and his voice was nearly cracking as he spoke. He's nervous, thought Iverson. This poor man—a dedicated employee who's now scared to death he's going to get fired.

"Mel, that was the question I was going to ask you. You've created one heck of team down there in assembly."

"And now they want to get rid of me," he responded, matter-of-factly.

"These things happen, Mel. I've seen it many times before."

That was a total lie, thought Iverson. I've never seen anything like this before, but if it will keep Mel upbeat, it's a lie I can live with. I've got to create the image that I know what I'm doing here.

"So, the times before, what'd you do?" asked Mel, innocently, genuinely curious. He was less nervous now.

"Well, no two situations are exactly the same . . ." That was a bad start. He began again, "Mel, I think you should . . . ." He stopped; that was even worse. He didn't want to give Mel an order, he wanted Mel to have a say in this decision. Mel's grey eyes were staring at him; Mel was hanging on his every word. Iverson gathered himself, picked up a mug of coffee, and took a long sip. The coffee was cold—he'd picked up the wrong mug! That coffee was at least a week old; surely it had mold growing in it. He grimaced and tried to swallow it all the way down, not wanting to make a scene while poor Mel was sitting across from him. The cold liquid lingered in the back of his mouth as if in a debate about whether to proceed downward or return to the surface. He could feel his gag reflex tittering on the edge of acti-vation. He concentrated: swallow, swallow, swallow—for god's sake don't spray coffee all over Mel—swallow, swallow, swallow. He gulped hard twice. On the second gulp, he could feel the brackish liquid finally begin its descent.

"Are you all right?" asked Mel.

"I guess it just went down the wrong pipe," lied Iverson. He let out a short cough for effect. What did you get from drinking moldy coffee? Nothing serious, he hoped.

"Where were we, Mel?"

"You were going to tell me what you wanted to do in regard to this situation with the team."

"What I want to do is describe what I see as the options. I want you to decide which one will be best for you and the team." This was a good approach. Iverson continued, "First, we could say 'no' to them, that you're the team leader and that they need to respect that. Option two would be to say 'yes' and allow them to operate without a team leader. I'd put you on a special project and keep an eye on their performance to make sure it doesn't slip. You'd be contributing to the organization working on the special project, and the team could pursue its goal of operating as a self-managed team. There may be other options, but these two seem the most readily obvious."

"John, I just don't want to lose my job."

"Mel, that's not one of the options." Iverson could see him lighten up a bit. He even smiled.

"So, which option do you like?" said Iverson.

"I think the best scenario is for me to leave the team. I won't be resentful. Maybe they will even see a role for me down the road."

"I think you're right, Mel; that's how these things usually work out. After a while, the team sees how valuable and necessary the leader role is." Another white lie—he didn't have a clue as to how it "usually worked out." At least Mel was looking and feeling better, and maybe, just maybe, a potential disaster had been avoided.

Survivor Tips

To avoid getting devoured by a Tyrannosaurus team, consider the following tips.

Authority Cycle

The relationship between a designated leader (whether he or she is titled as a supervisor, manager, or team leader) and the members of the team follows a predictable path (see Figure 11.1). The first stage is one of dependence—the team is dependent on the manager for authority, information, resources, and skill development. As the manager begins transferring decision-making and problem-solving authority, providing additional business and operational information, bringing in needed resources, and providing training and development support, the teams moves on to the second stage of development—counterdependence.

During the second stage, counterdependence, the team will tend to rebel against the authority figure. Often, this stage is characterized by confusion over roles and responsibilities. Team members may seek to absorb virtually all managerial responsibilities and may question the value of the manager's role. In the extreme, the team may even seek to get the manager removed from the team.

During the counterdependent stage, it's very important for the manager to clarify the evolution of his or her role. Team members tend to think of roles—particularly management roles—in terms of what was done in the past rather than what could be done in the future. If the manager takes attendance,

Figure 11.1   Authority Cycle in Groups

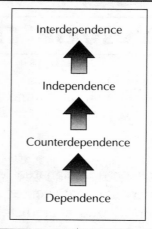

coordinates the vacation schedule, sets the work assignments, gives feedback on performance results, and addresses performance problems, without effectively defining how he or she can best contribute in the future, team members will begin to see the manager as redundant and unnecessary as the team absorbs many of his or her former responsibilities.

In the third, or independence, phase of the authority cycle, the team attempts to operate independently of its manager. Team members largely ignore the authority figure and generally operate without his or her input.

Ideally, the team will evolve all the way to the fourth phase: interdependence. During this phase, the unique contributions that the leader can bring to the team are fully recognized and appreciated. At this point, the team and the manager or leader have developed a high level of trust and rapport and work together effectively.

The tendency for team members to rebel or to resist the influence and guidance of the designated leader is a natural part of team development. Team leaders, supervisors, managers, or anyone else who is attempting to lead a team should be aware of this tendency. The best strategy for overcoming team rebellion is to focus time and energy on describing how the roles and responsibilities of the team and of the team leader will expand in the future.

Positive Pressure

Peer pressure can, and often does, act as a tremendous positive force in developing and sustaining teams. This force can help ensure that team members are performing at an acceptable level, reinforce important ground rules and team discipline, and provide a sense of belonging and esprit de corps. However, when not channeled properly, peer pressure can lead to equally destructive consequences: nonacceptance of diverse viewpoints, formation of combative cliques or factions, and confrontational feedback.

Having a clear and well-thought-out process in place gives the team several advantages.

Defining the steps that the team will follow when addressing difficult issues, before it ever has to face them can help to ensure peer pressure serves as a positive force. The team should define in advance how it will deal with issues such as:

■ Performance problems.
■ Individuals who break team ground rules.
■ Safety violators.
■ Attendance and tardiness problems.

---

1. By taking the time up front to design how the team will deal with these issues, the team can make sure its process is consistent with any legal or company policy considerations. This consistency is particularly important in dealing with employee performance problems in a fair and professional manner.

2. Everyone on the team knows what the steps are and what happens. Where there is a formal process, there are no surprises.

3. A well-designed process lessens the likelihood of a knee-jerk, emotion-filled response.

4. This process helps preserve the dignity and self-esteem of all of the individuals involved.

Taming Tyrannosaurus

A team that appears to have become "too committed"—its arrogance and tactics have actually become a destructive force within the organization—is often the result of the team members' having made the mistake of assuming that the end can justify the means.

When members of a team raid another group for equipment, break into a database to acquire confidential information, or verbally assault a poor-performing teammate, they are assuming

---

The central obligation of any high performing team is to transfer knowledge, skill and capability to other departments, groups and individuals within the organization. If the team is not fulfilling this role it may actually be hurting the overall performance of the organization regardless of what the team's individual performance numbers seem to indicate.

that the bottom-line results they will achieve by taking these drastic actions more than justify any pain or suffering they create along the way. This concept is the Tyrannosaurus team mentality: periphery destruction is acceptable as long as strong team results are achieved.

To tame a Tyrannosaurus team, work with its members to:

1. Recognize and accept that a key part of its role is to transfer learning, knowledge, and capability to others.
2. Recognize that achieving results by hurting the performance of another department, the integrity of a system, or the feelings of an individual is not success. All of these actions hurt the overall capabilities of the organization as a whole.

Although a highly committed team can be a huge asset, if its energies are not focused properly, it can become an equally huge liability.

Part III

The Escape

Chapter 12

꙰ ꙰ ꙰ ꙰

The Team Puzzle

As a boy, I was fascinated by a puzzle game I received for my birthday. The game consisted of seven differently shaped blocks that, when put together correctly, formed a small cube. One night, while working on the puzzle, I asked my father why it was so difficult. After all, I noted, the instruction book claimed that there were hundreds of different combinations that would lead to a correct configuration of the cube. My father smiled, "What they don't tell you is that there are thousands of ways to get it wrong!"

Although many pathways will lead to highly effective teams, a far greater number of trails lead to underutilization, problems, and even disaster. The key to success is to understand both what makes teams succeed and what potentially makes them fail. Team literature tends to focus on the success stories—which are critical but serve as only one piece of the puzzle. An understanding of why teams fail is as important as an appreciation of the nuances that allow them to succeed.

The problem, as it was with my boyhood blocks, is the sheer complexity of solving the puzzle. How can we quickly identify and rule out pathways that could ultimately lead toward failure and, with equal dedication and speed, identify the characteristics that need to be in place for success? To be successful in a quest to develop and sustain a high-performing team, we must understand how the team traps are set and what critical disciplines will help us avoid traps altogether.

The Three Failures

Although there are many ways a team can become trapped and end up in a downward spiral, the mechanism that triggers ineffectiveness is related to one of these fundamental failures:

1. A failure of team *leadership*—lack of: support, consistency of direction, vision, budget, and/or resources.
2. A failure of team *focus*—lack of clarity about: team purpose, roles, responsibilities, strategies, and goals.
3. A failure of team *capability*—lack of: critical skill sets, knowledge, ongoing learning, and development.

Trap Diagnosis

The concept may seem unreasonably simple, but every common team trap has, at its genesis, a failure in one of just three factors: leadership, focus, or capability. Because of the simplicity of the model, diagnosing the underlying cause of a trap is relatively easy.

Leadership
A failure in leadership can occur for a variety of reasons: a lack of support, a manager who is politically naive, an executive

decision to lay off employees in order to shore up short-term profits, or a poorly-thought-out succession plan. Regardless of how the failure originates, its impact on the organization can be traumatic—even devastating.

The simple truth is that teams cannot exist without strong leadership and support. Team-based work systems run counter to so many traditional management assumptions and practices that a lack of support and commitment from someone in a leadership role is the kiss of death for the team.

Focus

At the most fundamental level, all team members should be able to answer three basic questions.

1. Why does our team exist?
2. How will we know if we are successful?
3. What is my role in helping the team achieve success?

Surprisingly, many groups are formed into "teams" but the members cannot give a reasonable answer to any of these fundamental questions. Even in the current information age, many employees receive so little communication from management that they cannot even describe what product they are building!

Teams are not nocturnal—they cannot survive in a state of information darkness. A team can only focus its energy on what it knows and understands. Effective team functioning requires a open, free flow of information.

Capability

Having the technical skills necessary to perform a job is obviously important. In a team-based workplace, having strong interpersonal, decision-making, and problem-solving skills is equally important. Because of the ever changing demands placed on the team, members need to be continually developing new areas of

Figure 12.1 Leadership, Focus, and Capability Pyramid

Traps that lead to a decline in team effectiveness typically are related to one of three factors: leadership, focus, or capability. Each of these three factors requires a different strategy to overcome the trap.

Leadership

Lack of: support, consistency of direction, vision, budget, and resources.

Improvement strategies:

- Plan events to ensure demonstrated leadership support.
- Increase availability of budget and resources.
- Increase communication and contact with leader.
- Change leadership.

Focus

Lack of clarity about: team purpose, roles, responsibilities, strategies, and goals.

Improvement strategies:

- Establish and clarify team charter.
- Clarify boundary conditions.
- Ensure open channels for communication and information transfer.
- Clarify team member roles.
- Establish regular team meetings.

Capability

Lack of: critical skill sets, knowledge, ongoing learning, and development.

Improvement strategies:

- Provide appropriate education and training.
- Establish a team development plan.
- Establish individual development plans.
- Reflect on how group processes can be improved.
- Regularly assess team effectiveness.

knowledge and new skill sets. In fact, the ability of a team to improve its performance hinges on the ability of its members to continually apply new learning.

A team that lacks basic capabilities (e.g., holding effective meetings, making decisions, solving problems, and giving and receiving feedback) is easy prey for a trap. A team that has a good foundation in the basics but doesn't continually acquire and apply new knowledge will face an equally dismal, trap-filled future.

The leadership, focus, and capability pyramid shown in Figure 12.1 gives us a quick and easy way to diagnose the underlying cause of a team trap and implies specific strategies for addressing it. If, for example, the trap we face is related to a failure of capability, our corrective action should include developing increased team knowledge and skill. Depending on the issue being addressed, corrective actions might include a team training session, or the addition of a new team member who is proficient in a critical skill area that the team lacks. Similarly, if the trap was diagnosed as being the result of a failure to focus, the corrective action would emphasize gaining clarity on priorities, boundary conditions, goals, or principles.

Toward a Trap-Proof Team

Strong team *leadership*, a clear sense of *focus*, and the continual development of new *capability* among team members are necessary to "trap-proof" a team. Developing this level of leadership, focus, and capability requires learning, practice, and commitment. In a word, trap-proofing demands *discipline*.

Chapter 13

꧁ ꧁ ꧁ ꧁

The Team Disciplines

Athletes who are training for the Olympics commonly work out for 8 to 10 hours a day, 6 times a week. This level of dedication is equally common among world-class musicians, artists, and business and political leaders. To attain excellence in a chosen field, a person must be capable of extraordinary devotion and a high level of self-discipline. Oddly, it is rarely suggested that members of work teams must also commit to a high level of personal discipline in order to achieve high performance.

If we accept the premise that world-class performance, in any endeavor, requires practice and dedication, it is surprising the haphazard way many teams are formed, educated, and developed. This sloppiness is especially surprising in light of the importance that the team concept now enjoys in business circles. Yet, despite its prominence as a topic of discussion among organizational leaders, development of teams is allocated only a tiny fraction of corporate resources.

The Team Ethic

Will highly effective teams emerge routinely once a team structure is in place and team members have been identified? The answer is no. As previous chapters in this book have illustrated, many complexities are involved in the creation of high-performing teams—complexities that are often left unaddressed or are altogether ignored.

High-performing teams are not necessarily smarter or more innovative than low-performing groups—rather, the characteristic that differentiates the high performers is a willingness to do the unglamorous, often tedious work of setting agendas, giving feedback, reviewing decisions, and coaching peers.

The ethic of working on—and continuously improving—core processes leads high-performing teams to vastly superior results.

Team Discipline

The ability of any team to achieve results is ultimately linked to 13 core disciplines.

A team discipline is *a learned and practiced set of behaviors and activities that leads to enhanced team performance.*

This definition has two critical elements. The first is the notion that team disciplines are *learned.* Reorganizing a department into teams will do little to engender teamwork if there is no corresponding education on how to work together effectively. For a director to send a troupe of actors onto a London stage without having any of them read the script for the performance would be unthinkable; yet many corporate "teams" are expected to achieve results with little more, in terms of education and guidance, than the memo that announced their initial formation. In essence, the team is operating without a script.

Learning the skills that enable teams to operate effectively is a significant undertaking. Core skills include clarity around the team's charter, how to make decisions, guidelines for interaction, how to solve problems, and strategies for dealing with conflict. If these skills are learned and developed, the team's potential grows. Without these skills, the team is trapped in a web of ambiguity and diminishing performance.

The second key element to the definition acknowledges that performance can only be improved through ongoing application of what has been learned—that is, it must be *practiced*. If new learning is not applied and practiced, it is soon forgotten. Teams are dynamic bodies that are never the same at the end of the workday—they have either gotten better through learning and practice or they have gotten worse because of a lack of these elements.

Thirteen Disciplines

Collectively, the 13 team disciplines are insurance against impending traps. By developing the disciplines, teams improve their performance and lessen the likelihood that they will fall victim to an unseen trip wire. Descriptions of the 13 critical team disciplines follow.

1. Customer-Centric Focus

Each member of the team knows who the customers are and what they expect from the products or services that the team provides. This linkage is so tight that the team develops the ability to anticipate customer needs or desires and can respond to them before the customer can even fully articulate the new requests. The effect that decisions, process or system changes, new policies or procedures, the development of new services, or the elimination of old services will have on the customer is considered first and foremost.

Teams that practice this discipline recognize that it goes beyond providing a service or building a product that is defect-free. That level of performance is common today. Teams that are truly customer-centric try to understand their customers' desires at a far deeper, almost metaphysical level. The goal is to create a product or provide a service that *profoundly affects the customer.*

In working toward this ultimate goal, the team uses a variety of methods, such as flowcharting customers and maintaining accurate customer profiles. By flowcharting, teams can identify their internal customers as well as the ultimate beneficiary of the product or service they provide (Figure 13.1). Through customer profiles, team members can maintain an accurate record of who their customers are and what they expect from the product or service the team provides (Figure 13.2).

2. Clarity of Purpose

This discipline recognizes the importance of team alignment to specific strategies, results, and measurements. On an ongoing basis, the team receives information and provides input toward vision, strategy, business objectives, procedures, policies, and measurements. Each team is highly focused and has a clear statement of its mission.

The importance of clarity of purpose cannot be overemphasized. Teams often flounder for the simple reason that they are unclear about their priorities and about where their energy should be focused. Developing a clear sense of team purpose begins with a charter or mission (see Figure 13.3 for an example). The mission statement answers the question "Why does

Figure 13.1 Simplified Customer Flowchart

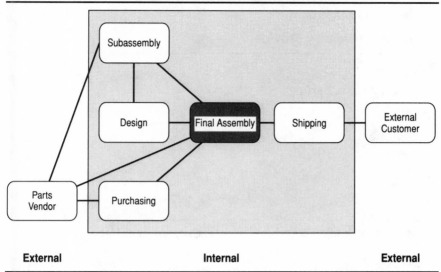

our team exist?" in clear, unambiguous terms. The mission statement must describe—at a minimum—the following:

- The team's primary purpose.
- The team's key customers (including internal customers, external customers, and end users).
- The key results or expectations the team is attempting to achieve.

A team displaying this discipline will regularly refer to the mission statement, particularly when attempting to define and prioritize projects.

3. Guiding Principles

Principles represent the core or guiding beliefs that are commonly held among team members. Principles help to keep team members focused—

Figure 13.2 Customer Profile Form

Company or team name:

Product/service they provide:

Key contact:

Key decision maker(s):

Location:

Telephone:

Fax:

E-mail:

Cellular:

Customer goals:	Current problems/pressures:

Contact log:

Figure 13.3   Mission Statement Example

The Business Staff exists for the purpose of improving the operating effectiveness of the Customer Service (CS) organization. The Business Staff achieves this mission by:

■ Solving problems, streamlining processes, eliminating barriers, and making decisions that directly impact CS.

■ Listening carefully to the needs of our customers and leading the change within the organization to ensure that these needs are met.

■ Actively supporting the CS teams.

■ Setting the overall strategy for the CS organization.

■ Being the guardians of team morale by taking on systems, processes, or structures that are having a negative effect on the ability of employees to get results.

The effectiveness of the Business Staff will be measured by:

■ Customer satisfaction results

■ Revenue growth

■ Employee morale index

---

particularly in decision-making situations—on what is in the best long-term interest of the organization. Many issues that face teams are inherently ambiguous and have trade-offs that may appear highly confusing. The discipline of establishing and utilizing principles keeps the team focused on those core values that are most important to uphold.

Teams that apply this discipline often refer to their guiding principles during discussions preceding difficult decisions. By elevating the level of the dialogue to consideration of how the different alternatives will reinforce or detract from the commonly held principles, the team can view the broader implications of a decision and develop an approach that is in the best long-term interest of the organization as a whole. Figure 13.4 is an example list of guiding principles.

Figure 13.4 Sample List of Guiding Principles

Our five core principles are:

1. *Customer focus.*

   In our decisions, we always consider, first and foremost, the effect they will have on our customers.

2. *Open communication.*

   Our interactions are open, honest, and direct.

3. *Commitments are sacred.*

   The commitments we make are always kept.

4. *Respect for others.*

   We treat all team members with dignity and respect.

5. *Team growth.*

   Teams will take on ever-increasing amounts of responsibility, authority, and accountability.

4. *Established and Recognized* **Boundary Conditions**

Boundary conditions describe the constraints and limitations that the team must consider and work within, when solving problems or making decisions. Boundary conditions provide the team with a framework that clarifies what the team can impact directly, without further management approval. Boundary conditions typically specify such things as expenditures, available resources, and time frame. Boundary conditions are intended to provide focus and clarity with regard to real constraints. Although they will not prevent teams from making mistakes, if properly set, boundary conditions will provide teams with a large degree of autonomy and will prevent "runaway" decisions that could result in business blunders.

Knowing up front what the real constraints and limitations are will help teams maximize their time and energy in coming up with solutions that will work. Teams that are fluent at this discipline will be knowledgeable about budgetary constraints, resource limitations, critical time lines and strategies. The team will work closely with its manager in order to recognize the boundary conditions that must be considered, given the specifics of the issue they are addressing. Figure 13.5 is an example of boundary conditions.

5. Effective Meeting and Interaction Habits

The effectiveness of interactions among team members can have a dramatic effect on team performance. Team meetings should be well planned, with a stated purpose, an agenda, clearly defined information requirements, a time frame, and projected outcomes. Clearly established operating guidelines should define the behaviors that are or are not acceptable during any inter-action team members have with one another.

Eighty percent of what determines the effectiveness of a meeting occurs before any of the participants arrive. Meetings are made or broken based on the premeeting work that goes into them. If a meeting is well planned and the participants know what roles they are to play and what behaviors are ex-pected from them, success is virtually guaranteed. Teams that develop this discipline have well-prepared meetings. One of the tools used to help prepare an effective meeting is PATIO.

Figure 13.5 Boundary Conditions—An Example

For the purposes of this redesign project, the team must work within the following constraints:

- $20,000 total budget.
- Redesign must be completed, and the line fully operational, by December 1996.
- The new design must be supported by the entire team.
- The new design must enhance customer service and team morale.
- The new design must be consistent with our "just-in-time" philosophy of eliminating waste.

PATIO is an acronym that stands for:

■ Purpose.
■ Agenda.
■ Time.
■ Information.
■ Outcomes.

PATIO provides a simple framework for team members who must plan and prepare for meetings.

6. Role Clarity

Role clarity helps team members recognize—in specific terms—how they are expected to contribute to the team. Clarification of roles helps provide focus to team members by stating what the minimum expectation is, but should not, in any way, limit the potential for team members to expand their roles in the future. Somewhat ironically, role clarity is a key element in preparing team members for role expansion and the acceptance of increased responsibilities and role ambiguity. This discipline requires teams regularly to discuss the roles of team members and to assess what changes are necessary, given the conditions the business faces.

The roles necessary for a team to operate effectively exist at three levels. The first level is understanding what responsibilities and knowledge need to be *common* among all team members. These common elements might include such things as specific types of business knowledge, core interpersonal skills (e.g., giving and receiving feedback), essential team skills (e.g., holding effective meetings and making consensus decisions), and technical skills (the minimum level of technical competence all members must have). The second level is the *unique* skills and knowledge a limited number of individuals on the team currently have. The unique components include those roles that are not practical to cross-train but are necessary for the team to achieve its goals. The third level is *development*. The roles defined under the development category are those areas where the team needs to be proficient but has no current capability.

7. Clear Accountability for Action

Within a team-based work system, there is strong individual and team accountability. When action items are created, a clear definition of who will do what by when is established. Once an individual has volunteered to take an action on a project, the team norm is that the commitment is met. The types of decisions that require full team support versus those decisions that must be made immediately by individuals or a subgroup are clarified.

Any time a decision is made, an action plan is developed that specifies the nature of the action (what), the person responsible (who), the time frame (when), and any resources that will be required (resources). The action plans are reviewed at each team meeting, and the team holds the team members who are assigned action items accountable for the results. See Figure 13.6 for an action planning template.

8. Decision-Making Mechanisms

Team members understand when they are empowered to take immediate action to address a customer concern or to handle an emergency situation. Team members also recognize issues that require the input and support of the entire team. When making a team decision, a process is followed in which the issue is clearly defined, full participation of the team is sought in discussing the issue, and a consensus is reached on what actions to take.

In upholding this discipline, the team has clearly defined instances where individual, on-the-spot decision making is appropriate versus decisions that are to be reviewed by the entire team. Consensus is the primary method for making group decisions. Team members recognize how consensus differs from other decision-making forms—including autocratic, democratic, and unanimous decision making. Team members realize

Figure 13.6　Action Planning Template

Who	What	When	Resources Required

that consensus does not mean every member of the group will necessarily think the best decision has been made. Consensus does ensure, however, that no one on the team is professionally violated by the decision and that all team members will support the implementation of the decision.

9. *Problem-Solving Mechanisms*

A critical skill for any effective team is its ability to solve problems. This discipline extends beyond merely identifying the existence of a problem or coming up with a preferred solution. It includes taking ownership for implementing a solution that eliminates the problem altogether. To accomplish this goal, teams must have a broad knowledge of problem-solving tools and methods.

High-performing teams are involved in all aspects of problem solving—from problem identification to developing possible solutions, making recommendations, ultimately taking ownership for implementing a solution, and monitoring how effectively the solution eliminates the problem. To effectively perform this role, all team members must be well versed in a common problem-solving process and be knowledgeable in how to apply a number of problem-solving tools.

10. *Performance Enhancement Feedback*

Team members are skilled at giving and receiving feedback. Whether its main focus is to develop, correct, or reward, this feedback is given in a way that ensures that the self-esteem of the recipient is preserved. In this discipline, a formal system is in place to receive feedback relating to team performance from customers, other teams, managers, and peers. Team members also provide direct feedback to their immediate manager.

In giving feedback, team members focus on the behavior that has been observed, and they refrain from making judgments or conclusions about the person's intent. Feedback is not only a tool for correcting negative behaviors. Among high-performing teams, the most common form of feedback is praise for noteworthy accomplishments. In addition, the team regularly solicits feedback about its performance from customers and other groups with which it regularly interacts. This feedback is often solicited through surveys and focus groups. The team is then diligent about reviewing and interpreting the feedback, taking action based on it, and reporting to the feedback providers what it has done. The five steps to providing effective feedback are:

1. Observe the behavior.
2. Give the feedback (when the time and place are appropriate).
3. Listen to the other perspective.
4. Develop an action plan.
5. Review progress.

11. *Work Redesign Methods Practiced*

Team members are highly focused on improving work methods and processes. On a regular basis, current methods are examined and ideas for improving effectiveness are assessed. In this way, work flow and work processes are redesigned on a regular basis.

In improving work design, team members first must have tremendous clarity about what their customers desire—regardless of whether they primarily serve internal or external customers. Once customer needs are known, a non-value-adding step can be defined as: any step in the work flow that does not ultimately help the team meet customers' desires. Once identified, the non-value-adding steps can be scrutinized and often eliminated. By eliminating these steps, the overall process becomes simplified and streamlined (see Figure 13.7).

12. *Learning and Continuous Development*

High-performing teams are able to learn from their past experiences and quickly transfer learning. A strong ethic exists that learning and its application are the only means to achieve continuous improvement. Team members

Figure 13.7 Work Flow Redesign

1. Define the customer.

2. Define the work design principles to be followed.

3. Identify the major transforms of the process.

4. Chart specific steps that occur in each transform.

5. Identify value-adding versus nonvalue-adding steps.

6. Identify ways to eliminate or minimize the impact of nonvalue-adding steps.

7. Develop an overall redesign.

regularly develop conceptual models and share practical experience that describes what they have learned and how this learning can be applied to solve issues or to exploit opportunities in the future.

The ability to reflect on past events, derive what was learned, and then apply that learning in the future is the essence of continuous improvement. In addition to learning from previous experiences, high-performing teams have development plans for individual members and for the team as an entity. Individual development plans are driven by skill and knowledge areas that will enhance each member's ability to make a greater contribution to team performance in the future. Team development plans are driven by those areas where the team, as a total unit, needs improved capability.

13. *Continuous Work and Development of the Disciplines*

Organizations are dynamic, ever-changing organisms. As a result, no organization is ever completely effective or truly performing at its optimal level of performance. The team regularly assesses its strengths and weaknesses in each of the disciplines and develops plans for improvement. Work on each discipline is ongoing.

To be effective over the long run, teams must learn, practice, and continually increase proficiency in each of the disciplines. The more embedded the discipline, the less likely that the team will succumb to one of three failures—a failure of *leadership*, of *focus*, or of *capability*—that ultimately can trigger a team trap.

A Difficult Journey

The transition from a traditionally structured organization to a team-based work system is a difficult undertaking. Many organizations underestimate the extent to which systems, processes, and roles are required to change as the transition unfolds. Invariably, the change requires the creation of a much flatter organization structure; the emergence of new information-sharing channels (e.g., organization-wide meetings and team meetings); the redesign of numerous systems and processes; the creation of team-based, rather than solely individual-based, performance measures; extensive training in team skills; a transferring of traditional "management" responsibilities to teams; and the development of the new team leadership role. The new organization that is created is fundamentally different from the one it replaced. All the old rules, processes, roles, and behaviors are altered. At every step during the transition, there is a potential for a team trap to derail it.

Overcoming a team trap requires quick diagnosis and responsive action planning. Avoiding a trap altogether requires discipline.

The Postmodern Challenge

Today's world is a very different place than it was a generation ago. For managers, the list of challenges is overwhelming:

- Competition coming from every part of the globe.
- Consumer demand compressing product life cycles from years to months.
- Tax revolts forcing governments to provide more services with less resources.
- Six-sigma quality performance quickly becoming the status quo.
- Technological change leading to hand-held computers that are more powerful than those that took up an entire room a decade ago.
- Employees expecting a high quality of work life.

The world managers face today is *postmodern*: it has changed so profoundly in the past 20 years that to describe it as merely *modern* seems wholly inadequate. Managers' success in these dynamic times requires a new philosophy and a new set of practices.

Without question, high-performance teams will be a central part of the postmodern manager's competitive arsenal. The performance advantage a team-based work system can provide is truly stunning. However, as we have learned, teams cannot be haphazardly thrown together. Team success hinges on the application of the 13 core disciplines.

For those who ignore the team disciplines, another fate lies ahead. In the corridors, conference rooms, offices, and work areas of organizations everywhere, the team traps are waiting.

Appendixes

Appendix A

A Quick Reference Guide to the Team Traps

The common team traps, presented in Chapter 2, are listed here in alphabetical order. Tips for overcoming each trap are provided for easy access and review.

- *Decision by default.* Teams that have a tendency to repeatedly table difficult decisions will find that their options become increasingly limited. Ironically, by hesitating, the team ultimately makes a decision—by default rather than by informed choice.

   —**Having a clear, concise definition of what consensus means is terribly important. By defining consensus, team members can recognize whether they can agree with the decision or whether there is a need for more discussion and analysis.**

   —**When facilitating a meeting where a team is attempting to reach a consensus, remember these guidelines:**

(1) clearly define the issue facing the team, (2) focus on similarities between positions, (3) ensure that there is adequate time for discussion, and (4) avoid conflict-reducing tendencies (e.g., voting).

—**A good question to pose when the team appears completely deadlocked is: "What are the consequences of not making a decision today?" or "What will be the default if we aren't able to decide?" Often, the consequences of not making any decision are more grave than taking some form of action.**

■ *Disruptive team member.* A disruptive member who is not dealt with firmly and effectively can damage the performance of the entire team. The reluctance of team members to provide direct and honest feedback to a peer can lead to frustration and declining performance.

—**Feedback needs to be nonjudgmental in content and it should focus on the observed behavior and the impact it had on the person who observed it. When giving feedback, do not guess as to the effect the behavior had on others—talk specifically from your own experience. "I" statements are very helpful. "When I observed you (*description of the behavior*), I felt (*description of the impact it had on you personally*)."**

—**In the high-performance team, giving constructive feedback that helps *correct* negative behaviors, *develop* new capabilities, and *reinforce* desired actions is the role of all team members.**

■ *Downsizing.* A decision to downsize as a way of shoring up short-term profits can destroy all the loyalty and commitment created by years of team development. The end result—as disgruntled workers look for new opportunities—can be a great "brain drain."

—The data are clear—don't make cuts to shore up the quarter's profits or to impress stockholders. Only cut when you have no other reasonable choice—when, quite literally, the survival of the business is hanging in the balance.

—The keys to a successful reorganization in troubled times are communication and dialogue. Communicate why changes must be made, and engage in a dialogue in which alternatives can be openly explored with the people who will be directly affected by the change.

—Think of morale as a competitive advantage that is as important to maintain as state-of-the-art technology, superior customer service, total quality, or rapid time to market.

■ *Leader abdication.* Some managers, in their sincere efforts to be good team leaders, make a serious mistake: they withdraw from their group and consciously avoid interacting with team members. They wrongly assume that the best way they can help the team become more self-directed is by personally becoming less involved.

—The leader's role is to work with the team, help develop its ability to use information, solve problems, and make decisions. As the team demonstrates an ability to make responsible decisions, it is granted ever-increasing levels of authority, resources, information, accountability, and skill development.

—Based on where the team falls on the maturity gauge, define the team's limits. Not every decision is open for debate nor can every penny in the budget be spent at the team's whim. The leader must define the real limits and constraints.

—Using the right or wrong phrase will not, in itself, lead to disaster, but "self-management" is a loaded term—so why use it? "High-performance team" is a better phrase because it describes the outcomes the team is attempting to achieve rather than the means to achieve them.

—Once the team has described its rationale for the decision, calmly explain your concerns. It's important to avoid getting emotional and to stick to the facts at hand.

—The tendency for team members to rebel or even resist the influence and guidance of the designated leader is a natural part of team development. Team leaders, supervisors, managers, or anyone who is attempting to lead a team should be aware of this tendency. The best strategy for overcoming rebellion is to focus time and energy on describing how the roles and responsibilities of the team and of the leader will expand in the future.

■ *Participation gimmickry.* Gimmicks to increase employee involvement and participation—like suggestion boxes—can actually have the opposite effect. When individuals are rewarded for contributing suggestions through cash payouts, there is little incentive for team members to work together to address problems and implement solutions.

—As a general guideline, during the transition to a team-based workplace, any suggestion box system that already exists should be discontinued. The odds are that the continued use of the suggestion box will serve to stunt the development of the team as an effective improvement-generating unit, particularly if recognition and rewards for suggestions are given only to

individuals. In the extreme, idea stealing may occur where one individual gets a payout for an idea that was first articulated by another team member. This suggestion misuse perpetuates a sense of distrust among members of the team and reduces their will- ingness to openly share their ideas.

—**Cash payouts in suggestion systems are based on an outdated perspective of what motivates people— money, alone, does not motivate. In fact, intrinsic fac- tors—having a say in how to perform the job, having autonomy in choosing a work schedule, being directly involved in making decisions and solving problems, and receiving feedback about job performance—will create far higher levels of personal motivation than a small cash payout.**

■ *Political suicide.* Companies, government agencies, academic institutions, and even nonprofit organizations are inherently political. Ignoring or defying the organization's political side can lead to some harsh consequences, particularly if those in power are publicly challenged or ridiculed by over zealous team members.

—**By giving grace to past achievements, you are seen as building on strengths rather than attempting to tear apart weaknesses. There is a subtle but profound dif- ference here. Those who have a vested interest in maintaining the status quo will pose far less resistance if you are perceived as setting a course that builds on their achievements rather than a course that chal- lenges the validity of—and even discredits—their past decisions.**

—**Team leaders must be willing to take on barriers that are hurting team performance, but they need to do so** in a manner that is thoughtful and carefully planned, and that builds credibility and support within the management ranks.

—If you are going to take a position that may appear to be politically unacceptable, remain focused on what is in the best interest of the business—even if this position may ultimately cause some grumbling among the management hierarchy. Always convey your message calmly, in matter-of-fact terms, so that you clearly convey that you are interested, only in business performance, not in political gain. And, perhaps the most important point of all, *take action*. By hesitating, you are damaging your personal integrity.

■ *Poor teamwork habits.* When a team operates as a group of individuals rather than as a tight, cohesive unit, little, if any, synergy is created when team members collaborate on projects. Meetings tend to be ineffective, with members often not showing up or coming in late. The feeling of the majority is: "My real work is too important for me to take the time to be a team member."

—If the team has made a bad decision, sit down with the team and review the decision, emphasizing what can be learned from the experience. It is important to avoid blaming anyone or pulling rank. Just talk the team through the impact the decision had, and let the team members explore what they learned and what actions can be taken to ensure that the mistake does not recur.

—Teams need to choose consciously the ground rules by which they want to operate. These ground rules should define such things as how meetings are best conducted, how decisions are most effectively made, how leadership can be shared within the group, and how feedback is given to team members in a constructive manner.

—The effectiveness of a meeting is largely determined before the participants enter the conference room—the key is in the planning. Poorly planned meetings inevitably lead to poor results. Meetings designed using the PATIO process will be more efficient and effective. Further, getting the agenda out to participants in advance can go a long way toward eliminating frustrations caused by unprepared or late participants.

—Ideally, all team members would be equally capable of getting the team refocused and the meeting back on track, once a disruption has occurred. This, in fact, should be the long-term goal—creating a team fully capable of self-regulation. Most teams, however, rely on the meeting facilitator to take the lead in dealing with problems that arise. For this reason, it's important that the facilitator has some strategies for dealing with the disruptions he or she is likely to encounter.

■ *Short-term focus.* Failure to see the "big picture" can lead a team to pursue strategies and make decisions that help pump up its own performance numbers but leave the rest of the organization in shambles. Not having the information that allows seeing the forest rather than the trees can lead to suspect plans and poorly reasoned decisions.

—Ensure that team members have a base level of knowledge about the organization, its goals, and the way it is structured.

—Before implementing a decision that could have a direct effect on another team or department, the decision should be reviewed and feedback should be

sought from the group that will be affected. Often, new insights will emerge that may significantly alter the original decision.

■ *Successionless planning.* The important role that one individual—a champion for change—can play in developing a high-performance team is often underestimated. If a team is newly formed or still in its relative infancy, losing its leader to a transfer, a promotion, a new job, or retirement can mark the beginning of the team's demise—particularly if the replacement brings in a management philosophy that runs counter to team development.

—**Make sure that a long-term perspective can be maintained and a high degree of leadership continuity is in place.**

—**When making a leadership change in an organization, determine whether the new manager is going to be a good fit with the team culture.**

■ *Team arrogance.* A team can become so focused on achieving its own goals that it does not consider the impact its actions may have on other groups or organizations. Outsiders see the team as arrogant and ruthless. Insiders see the team as effective and misunderstood. Overall, the team's belief in its own superiority has a detrimental effect on the performance of the organization as a whole.

—**An effective coaching approach is to describe the decision from the viewpoints of all of the involved parties. This approach can help demonstrate that a decision that seems like a good idea from one perspective can look like a complete disaster from another vantage point. By describing the different perspectives in detail, team members will begin to develop a greater appreciation and understanding of the** interdependence that exists within the organization, and the importance of taking this interdependence into consideration during decision making.

—A central part of the team leader's role is to develop effective linkages between his or her team and the rest of the organization. If the team leader, either purposely or accidentally, sends a message that the team doesn't value the opinions of others or that the rest of the organization is "backward" and "ineffective," he or she will hurt the creation of these critical linkages.

—A central obligation of any high-performing team is to transfer knowledge, skill, and capability to other departments, groups, and individuals within the organization. If the team is not fulfilling this role, it may actually be hurting the overall performance of the organization, regardless of what the team's individual performance numbers seem to indicate.

■ *Undefined accountability.* In this trap, a team may regularly make decisions on which no subsequent action is ever taken. Members are then frustrated by the collective lack of accountability. In instances when action is taken and the execution is poor or a mistake is made, no one takes responsibility. It is rarely clear who is accountable for specific action items, and when an action item is designated as the responsibility of the entire team, nothing happens.

—Every time a decision is made or an action is agreed to, make sure that the team has clearly identified *who* will do *what* by *when* and what *resources* will be required.

—At the beginning of each meeting, review the status of any action items that were previously assigned. Encourage team members to assume the responsibility of

holding their peers accountable for completing the action items they've been assigned.

■ *Varied team member contributions.* A few members may be carrying the load for everyone else on the team. Those who are putting in the longer hours and making the greater contributions become increasingly frustrated with their "lower" contributing teammates.

—**To ensure that peer pressure serves as a positive force, the team should define the steps it will follow when addressing difficult issues, before it ever has to face them. The team should define, in advance, how it will deal with issues such as:**

Performance problems.

Individuals who break team ground rules.

Safety violators.

Attendance and tardiness problems.

Appendix B

Survey of the Thirteen Disciplines

To what extent does your team currently display the following disciplines?

1. Customer-Centric Focus

Each member of the team knows who the customers are and what they expect from the products or services that the team provides. This linkage is so tight that the team develops the ability to anticipate customer needs or desires and can respond to them before the customer can even fully articulate the new requests. The effect that decisions, process or system changes, new policies or procedures, the development of new services, or the elimination of old services will have on the customer is considered first and foremost.

1	2	3	4	5	6	7
Never			Sometimes			Always

2. Clarity of Purpose

The team is aligned with specific strategies, results, and measurements. On an ongoing basis, the team receives information and provides input toward vision, strategy, business objectives, procedures, policies, and measurements. Each team is highly focused and has a clear statement of its mission.

1	2	3	4	5	6	7
Never			Sometimes			Always

3. Guiding Principles

Principles represent the core or guiding beliefs that are commonly held among team members. Principles help to keep team members focused—particularly in decision-making situations—on what is in the best long-term interest of the organization. Many issues that face teams are inherently ambiguous and have trade-offs that may appear highly confusing. The discipline of establishing and utilizing principles keeps the team focused on those core values that are most important to uphold.

1	2	3	4	5	6	7
Never			Sometimes			Always

4. Established and Recognized Boundary Conditions

Boundary conditions describe the constraints and limitations that the team must consider and work within, when solving problems or making decisions. Boundary conditions provide the team with a framework that clarifies what the team can impact directly, without further management approval. Boundary conditions typically specify such things as expenditures, available resources, and time frame. Boundary conditions are intended to provide focus and clarity with regard to real constraints. Although they will not prevent teams from making mistakes, if properly set, boundary conditions will provide teams with a large degree of autonomy and will prevent "runaway" decisions that could result in business blunders.

1	2	3	4	5	6	7
Never			Sometimes			Always

5. Effective Meeting and Interaction Habits

The effectiveness of interactions among team members can have a dramatic effect on team performance. Team meetings should be well planned, with a stated purpose, an agenda, clearly defined information requirements, a time frame, and projected outcomes. Clearly established operating guidelines should define the behaviors that are or are not acceptable during any interaction team members have with one another.

1	2	3	4	5	6	7
Never			Sometimes			Always

6. Role Clarity

Role clarity helps team members recognize—in specific terms—how they are expected to contribute to the team. Clarification of roles helps provide focus to team members by stating what the minimum expectation is, but should not, in any way, limit the potential for team members to expand their roles in the future. Somewhat ironically, role clarity is a key element in preparing team members for role expansion and the acceptance of increased responsibilities, and role ambiguity. This discipline requires that teams regularly discuss the roles of team members and assess what changes are necessary, given the conditions the business faces.

1	2	3	4	5	6	7
Never			Sometimes			Always

7. Clear Accountability for Action

Within a team-based work system, there is strong individual and team accountability. When action items are created, a clear definition of *who* will do *what* by *when* is established. Once an individual has volunteered to take action on a project, the team norm is that the commitment is met. The types of decisions that require full team support versus those decisions that must be made immediately by individuals or a subgroup are clarified.

1	2	3	4	5	6	7
Never			Sometimes			Always

8. Decision-Making Mechanisms

Team members understand when they are empowered to take immediate action to address a customer concern or to handle an emergency situation. Team members also recognize issues that require the input and support of the entire team. When making a team decision, a process is followed in which the issue is clearly defined, full participation of the team is sought in discussing the issue, and a consensus is reached on what actions to take.

1	2	3	4	5	6	7
Never			Sometimes			Always

9. Problem-Solving Mechanisms

A critical skill for any effective team is its ability to solve problems. This discipline extends beyond merely identifying the existence of a problem or coming up with a preferred solution. It includes taking ownership for implementing a solution that eliminates the problem altogether. To accomplish this goal, teams must have a broad knowledge of problem-solving tools and methods.

1	2	3	4	5	6	7
Never			Sometimes			Always

10. Performance Enhancement Feedback

Team members are skilled at giving and receiving feedback. Whether its main focus is to develop, correct, or reward, this feedback is given in a way that ensures that the self-esteem of the recipient is preserved. In this discipline, a formal system is in place to receive feedback relating to team performance from customers, other teams, managers, and peers. Team members also provide direct feedback to their immediate manager.

1	2	3	4	5	6	7
Never			Sometimes			Always

11. Work Redesign Methods Practiced

Team members are highly focused on improving work methods and processes. On a regular basis, current methods are examined and ideas for improving its effectiveness are assessed. In this way, work flow and work processes are redesigned on a regular basis.

1	2	3	4	5	6	7
Never			Sometimes			Always

12. Learning and Continuous Development

High-performing teams are able to learn from their past experiences and quickly transfer learning. A strong ethic exists that learning and its application are the only means to achieve continuous improvement. Team members regularly develop conceptual models and share practical experience that describes what they have learned and how this learning can be applied to solve issues or to exploit opportunities in the future.

1	2	3	4	5	6	7
Never			Sometimes			Always

13. Continuous Work and Development of the Disciplines

Organizations are dynamic, ever-changing organisms. As a result, no organization is ever completely effective or truly performing at its optimal level of performance. The team regularly assesses its strengths and weaknesses in each of the disciplines and develops plans for improvement. Work on each discipline is ongoing.

1	2	3	4	5	6	7
Never			Sometimes			Always

Summary Sheet for Survey of the Thirteen Disciplines

	Never		Sometimes				Always
	1	2	3	4	5	6	7
1. Customer-centric focus							
2. Clarity of purpose							
3. Guiding principles							
4. Established and recognized boundary conditions							
5. Effective meeting and interaction habits							
6. Role clarity							
7. Clear accountability for action							
8. Decision-making mechanisms							
9. Problem-solving mechanisms							
10. Performance enhancement feedback							
11. Work redesign methods practiced							
12. Learning and continuous development							
13. Continuous work and development of the disciplines							

About the Author

❧❧ ❧❧ ❧❧ ❧❧

Steven R. Rayner is founder of Rayner & Associates, Inc., a consulting and training firm that specializes in helping organizations implement high-performance work systems. Rayner has had extensive experience in "greenfield" and retrofit implementation efforts, as both a manager and consultant. A co-founder of the Belgard ■ Fisher ■ Rayner Alliance (BFR), Rayner is the primary author of the majority of the training materials offered by BFR.

Rayner's previous books on the subject of team-based work systems include *Recreating the Workplace: The Pathway to High-Performance Work Systems* (John Wiley & Sons, 1993) and, as a coauthor with K. Kimball Fisher and William Belgard, *Tips for Teams: A Ready Reference for Solving Common Team Problems* (McGraw-Hill, 1994).

Rayner's firm has worked with a number of corporations implementing high-performance practices, across North America and in the United Kingdom. His clients include IBM, Microsoft, Goodyear, and the State of Montana.

Rayner received a Bachelor of Arts from Lewis and Clark College and a Master of Science in organization development from Pepperdine University. He lives in the Pacific Northwest with his wife Colleen and sons Aidan, Dylan, and Riley.

For further information about Rayner and Associates:

Phone: 360-331-6773   5492 S. Harbor Ave.
Fax: 360-331-2047   P.O. Box 1164
Internet: rayner@whidbey.com Freeland, WA 98249

Index